A SMART ASSESSMENT METHODOLOGY TO MEASURE AND ANALYZE GOOGLE PLAY STORE

Rana M. Amir Latif
Muhammad Farhan
Khalid Hussain
Noor Zaman Jhanjhi
Mamoona Humayun

ELIVA PRESS

ELIVA PRESS

Rana M. Amir Latif
Muhammad Farhan
Khalid Hussain
Noor Zaman Jhanjhi
Mamoona Humayun

There are millions of apps on a regular basis, where the creators are uploading. The millions of consumers uninstall such applications without testing duplicated data. Such applications impact users' personal information which damages the confidence of the users in Google Store and also causes users to lose. In addition, there is some detail on such programs, which is provided on a play page. In this analysis job, with the aid of a crawler or scraper that is used to catalog, calculate and evaluate the millions of play store applications, we have scraped a Google play store dataset. We have specific types of applications after having collected the details regarding the applications from the play shop. Such apps are charged and optional, so we have a selection of different types of home apps so gaming applications. In this work we examined the quality of the applications by addressing different testing questions dependent on a dataset 's attributes. We also tested the causal constructs from databases, correlations, correlation, repeated trends, user feedback sentiment analysis, utilizing the different machine learning approaches that can support developers and consumers alike. We evaluated consumer feedback on game apps utilizing latent sentiment research, which is a text mining technique. We consider the determinants generating either user-positivity or hostility against game applications. We evaluated the association between the average measurement of the emotions and the average client ranking. We analyzed that in feedback sentiment analysis graph much of the application displaying the top ranking in the rating graph is not right. The fundamental explorations of this analysis are the association between free and paid application with download duration, commercials on free and paid applications with respect to a number of downloads, rating connection with quality. We also visualized the interaction between specific attributes from the play store data using multiple simulation methods that are more important to see how programs interact with each other depending on the different attributes.

Published: Eliva Press SRL

Address: MD-2060, bd.Cuza-Voda, 1/4, of. 21 Chişinău, Republica Moldova
Email: info@elivapress.com
Website: www.elivapress.com

ISBN: 978-1-952751-69-1

© Eliva Press SRL
© Rana M. Amir Latif, Muhammad Farhan, Khalid Hussain, Noor Zaman Jhanjhi, Mamoona Humayun
Cover Design: Eliva Press SRL
Cover Image by Freepik Premium

A SMART ASSESSMENT METHODOLOGY TO MEASURE AND ANALYZE GOOGLE PLAY STORE

[1]Rana M. Amir Latif
[2]Muhammad Farhan
[3]Khalid Hussain
[4]Noor Zaman Jhanjhi
[5]Mamoona Humayun
ranaamir10611@gmail.com[1]
farhansajid@gmail.com[2]
kusmani.utm@gmail.com[3]
noorzaman.jhanjhi@taylors.edu.my[4]
mahumayun@ju.edu.sa[5]

ABSTRACT

There are millions of apps on a regular basis, where the creators are uploading. The millions of consumers uninstall such applications without testing duplicated data. Such applications impact users ' personal information which damages the confidence of the users in Google Store and also causes users to lose. In addition, there is some detail on such programs, which is provided on a play page. In this analysis job, with the aid of a crawler or scraper that is used to catalog, calculate and evaluate the millions of play store applications, we have scraped a Google play store dataset. We have specific types of applications after having collected the details regarding the applications from the play shop. Such apps are charged and optional, so we have a selection of different types of home apps so gaming applications. In this work we examined the quality of the applications by addressing different testing questions dependent on a dataset 's attributes. We also tested the causal constructs from databases, correlations, correlation, repeated trends, user feedback sentiment analysis, utilizing the different machine learning approaches that can support developers and consumers alike. We evaluated consumer feedback on game apps utilizing latent sentiment research, which is a text mining technique. We consider the determinants generating either user-positivity or hostility against game applications. We evaluated the association between the average measurement of the emotions and the average client ranking. We analyzed that in feedback sentiment analysis graph much of the application displaying the top ranking in the rating graph is not right. The fundamental explorations of this analysis are the association between free and paid application with download duration, commercials on free and paid applications with respect to a number of downloads, rating connection with quality. We also visualized the interaction between specific attributes from the play store data using multiple simulation methods that are more important to see how programs interact with each other depending on the different attributes.

Keywords

Measurement and Analysis, CIRCOS Visualization, TF/ IDF, Rating, Google Play Store, Scraping, Semantic Analysis, Text Mining, Natural Language Processing, Machine Learning

Table of Contents

4

6

8

List of Figures

11

List of Tables

List of Abbreviation

NLP   Natural Language Processing
TF   Term Frequency
IDF   Invers Term Frequency
GP   Google Play
D3S   Driver Drowsiness Detection System
IAP   In Application Purchases
NB   Naïve Bayes

1 INTRODUCTION

1.1 Overview

Various third-party apps have been submitted to Google Play Store on a regular basis, and thousands of consumers log the personal details of their software on their smartphones, smart phones and other devices. Hundreds and thousands of developers have submitted millions of apps every day. The truth is that the upload material to the Play Store is completely unregulated and is accessed by millions of people (Yang et al., 2014). On the Google Play Store, though, there is some details regarding such programs. The biggest explanation is that there is a shortage of a robust method to test and explore Android devices. Different third-party users may use the source code in the program. Even Google does not have access to source code, the applications that are submitted as compressed binary packages directly to the Google play store (Crussell et al., 2012). To keep some from ripening, Google often sets other methods to store data indexing in Google play. For starters, play store data sets are limited to just 500 exploration applications of every search word or category through accessing the store's Internet interface. We provide details from the play sheet utilizing crawling and scraping strategies to analyze the knowledge from the Google Play sheet Material. For creeping, we have day-to-day knowledge even focused on the material that evolves every day. Therefore, we analyzed the quality of The App Store and Market on the basis of the Google Play Store (Bagnasco et al., 2015). We do have a number of various types of home apps and play apps since we have resurrected millions of applications from the play shop.

Our measurement and analysis helps developers to explore their information about the understanding Android applications development that what kind of content they should use in their applications on the basis of different attributes like ratings, score, downloads, reviews developer make decision that what kind of applications is more popular among the users and what is the reason that peoples like more that applications. Developers enhance the performance and efficiency of the applications. For an understanding Android application, we have performed different analysis and these measurements are more beneficial for developers and users also (Latif et al., 2020). At a specific scale, we have characterized the Google play store applications content. In this research work, we have measure and analyzed the relationship between free and paid application with download frequency, Advertisements on free and paid applications with downloads, ranking relationship with the price (Zhou et al., 2013).

Throughout our daily lives, we know that people mainly use android phones. Everybody is now utilizing an android device for a day, users are using numerous android devices, such as email, social networking, gaming and the apps. In the Android play store platform, you can select from over one million smartphone applications in various Handheld devices, although often the downloadable applications do not provide adequate functionality to bear it in mind (Ramzan et al., 2019). App store allows consumers to browse, purchase and install the ios update in a few taps. This app store offers mobile applications for free and paying access. The mobile applications are often regarded as "desktop phones (Tariq et al., 2019)." At a certain moment, an uneducated individual prepaid the device at downloaded a smartphone application. Once he downloaded the software, it was revealed to be an uneducated massage that he was offering the rating and that he did not realize what it was and that he was given the 5-star ranking. The rating of stars is not precise. Therefore, we use various data scraping methods to gather specific feedback on Google Play Store website. In such studies, we evaluate consumer feedback using numerous strategies of relational study (Latif et al., 2019a). With this tool, we will evaluate multiple android apps to pick the right one. You will use the feature to categorically equate two or more Android phones. For this feature, users will display the amount of optimistic, negative and neutral reviews. And consumers may often distinguish various applications by utilizing specific icons to display the link (Tallat et al., 2019). The consumer can show each program with a pie graph optimistic, negative and neutral feedback. The association between feedback and ratings is contained in this report and the association graph shows.

The essential task of natural language processing is classification of text strings or documents into different categories that are the part of this process, which depends upon the content of the string. Text classification has a variety of applications, including detection of user sentiments on comments or tweets, classification of an email as spam. Presently, text classification has gained vital importance for organizing online information (Goldberg, 2017). It is a ham, classifying blog posts in different categories, automating tagging of customer queries and so on. One of the major hiccups with text classification is the difficulty for the learner to generalize fairly with the help of little training data (Latif et al., 2019b). For example, most patient users can be satisfied by a news filtering service that required hundreds of days for training data. In this article we have used different algorithms and text classification techniques with android app reviews for different Google Play categories. We have improved the accuracy using the selected features (Genc-Nayebi and Abran, 2017).

Negative reviews express negativeness and positive reviews show users' positiveness with their experience. These written reviews show their opinions toward the games and describe users' experience related to game application (Aldabbas et al., 2020). User reviews therefore reflect user positiveness or negativeness in a more detailed manner than user ratings because written reviews are more informative. These reviews toward overall staying experience or some specific aspect of the application which the numbers are usually evaluated by users with the range from 1 to 10. The users of game applications utilizing electronic word of mouth to improve their application performance and generate demand. However, research comparing the type of determinants that create user positive and negative behavior and ranking their importance in leading user positiveness or negativeness is rare.

1.2   Google Play Scrapper

Node.js module to scrape application data from the Google Play store.
Installation
"npm install google-play-scraper"
Usage
Available methods:

- app: Retrieves the full detail of an application.
- list: Retrieves a list of applications from one of the collections at Google Play.
- search: Retrieves a list of apps that results of searching by the given term.
- developer: Returns the list of applications by the given developer name.
- suggest: Given a string returns up to five suggestion to complete a search query term.
- reviews: Retrieves a page of reviews for a specific application.
- similar: Returns a list of similar apps to the one specified.
- permissions: Returns the list of permissions an app has access to.
- categories: Retrieve a full list of categories present from dropdown menu on Google Play.

1.3   Google play Store

Google pay store is developed by the Google LLC, the Google play is the digital distribution service. For android operating system this service is serve as the officail paltform for the application store. This platform allow users to download and developers to upload the applications which is developed in a Andriod studio and these application is published through Google. The Google play store offers different services television programs, movies, books, offering music, books, music, offering and digital media store.(Latif et al., 2019a).

1.4   CIRCOS

CIRCOS is a package, which is used for visualizing the information and data. Data is visualized in a circular format that makes an ideal scenario to explore the objects and positions. The circular layout is more suitable and attractive. Besides, it is a good tool with high data to link ratio for publication quality infographics and illustrations; also, it has pleasant symmetric and richly layered data (Krzywinski et al., 2009).

1.5 Pie3D Chart

Pie3D climbs the value in x to guarantee that two PI, zeros and even NAs are achieved. This also reveals a blank plot, determines the structures used to draw on businesses and even requests the draw.tilted.business draws nearly any industry. Once tags are rendered usable, pie3D.label would be named to identify each field. The number of codes, codes and company colors will be equal to the set of values of x-ray as decorated. When the marks have been expanded, it can help to reduce or change the radius of this pastry. For all R artifacts, a shared intent. For more details on the parameter statements of the graphics. Plot.default should be used properly for uncomplicated distributed plots. Nevertheless, we find a background of different objects, e.g. functions, structures, details, densities things, techniques used, and so on (Kumar et al., 2001).

1.6 Text Mining

Text mining is also the method of obtaining high quality knowledge from language, that is to say the processing of data. The high-quality knowledge can be obtained by formulating patterns and developments by statistical methods. In the text mining process, the input is structured, the patterns are derived within structured data and the output is finally assessed and interpreted. Text mining knowledge typically applies to other value, innovation and significance combinations. Conventional activities of text mining include analysis of interactions, descriptive records, analyzes of emotions, creation of grit taxonomies, extraction of designs / entities, text clustering and categorization of messages (Aggarwal and Zhai, 2012).

1.7 Sentiment Analysis

Sentimental insight is also classified as viewpoint mine or sentiment AI. The analysis of emotions often includes the use of subjective knowledge, research affective condition, quantification, sampling, biometrics, electronic linguistics, text interpretation, and natural linguistical processing. Sentiment research is mainly utilized for consumers, for example consumer manuals, electronic and web networking, as well as survey results varying from advertisement and patient relations and clinical medicine.

1.8 Natural Language Processing

The main work of the natural language processing (NLP) is how the program computers process and analyzed the large amount of natural language data. The NLP is the subfield of artificial intelligence and computer science which is concerned with the interaction of between human and computers.

1.8.1 Bigram

The bigram is the set of tokens that usually are phrases, letters and syllables. The n=2 is the n-gram, the bigram is used for basic mathematical study of text in numerous uses, including voice recognition, cryptography and machine linguistics (Li et al., 2015).

1.8.2 Trigram

In the fields of probability and computational linguistics we have used n-grams. In n-gram we have n=3 which is used in natural language processing for performing statistical analysis.

1.8.3 N-gram

The n-gram is the continuous series of n objects from the stated text or speech sample. The elements are the code foundation sets, phrases, characters and syllables. If the things are words, the n-gram is sometimes called shingles (Pagán et al., 2016).

1.8.4 TF/IDF

The term frequency / inverse document frequency (TF/IDF) is also referred to as the numerical statistics which show the value of a word in a list. For app simulation, Text Mining and knowledge retrieval analysis the TF/IDF is used as a weighting element.

1.9 Different Machine Learning Algorithm use for Analysis

Machine learning is a mathematical process and a theoretical analysis of algorithms to successfully execute a given function, by utilizing specific commands, but without depending on computer machine trends in order. The artificial intelligence sub-set (AI), is Machine Learning (ML). To carry out the process without the explicit programming of reference databases such as training data in order to render projections or judgments, the ML is to construct a mathematical model.

1.9.1 Random Forest Algorithm

Classifier of Random Forests is the class of all approaches specifically constructed for the vine. This relies on the random sorting of data and a random choice of variables a set of decision tree.

1.9.2 Logistic Regression Algorithm

In statistics, the logistic product can be a trusted statistical version which, in its basic type that runs on the logistic functionality to simulate a binary determining factor; lots complex extensions exist. Back in regression investigation, logistic regression will be estimating the parameters of the logistic version; it is an application of both binomial regressions.

1.9.3 Naïve Bayes Multinomial NB Algorithm

Naive Bayes is used to identify large dimensional data sets. It means that a single function exists independently of other features. Models and forecasts are easy to make.

1.10 Correlation Coefficient Algorithm

We measured the association between the ranking and the evaluation sentiment study. The association graph is displayed. The relation between two or more variables is correlation. The association factor varies from -1 to 1. When our reaction is not within context, our reaction is inaccurate. Therefore, the 0 is no correlation, because if the -1 is the association, the negative correlation is a good correlation, the +1 is the best positive correlation and the 0 to 0 to +1 is the highest degree of interaction.

1.10.1 Positive Correlation

The condition is, if one variable raises the second variable and if one reduces, the second variable declines. The connection is positive.

1.10.2 Negative Correlation

It is a situation where if the second variable rises and the second variable declines then it always reduces the second variable. This is a negative interaction.

1.10.3 No Correlation

No correlation means that there is no positive or negative increase for every increase.

1.11 Reviews Positiveness and Negativeness

1.11.1 Positiveness

User positiveness may be explained as an assessment which is made by comparison among two as users' expectation about app and user's experience. Index of user's positives is an efficient way for measurement of user's positive attitude about game applications. User's positive attitude most of the time plays a significant role in increasing demand for any game applications, which may be a source of improvement in game performance with higher efficiency. There are many key features which may lead to user's positiveness; the research found seven main factors that positively manipulate user's positive attitude overall like as game enjoyment, efforts for gameplay, Offers in games and Graphics.

1.11.2 Negativeness

Fewer studies discuss user negativeness toward the application of game with a comparison of positiveness. Though leading factors of user's negativeness discussion are necessary because they are diversifying than their leading factor of user positiveness. Some studies investigate some leading factors to user negativeness such as negativeness, insecurity, uncertainty, unmet expectations, and services poor quality. Daytripper service with negativeness may manipulate with the anger emotion, disappointed and may lead to the consequence such as negative reviews, complaint, negative attitude, and negative electronic words of mouth. Moreover, users whom unsatisfied tends to go away their current game application to some other game application, they use negativeness voice tendency for releasing their tension, gain sympathy from other users, and obtain compensation. It is necessary to game application's performance that to Keeping holds on users and encouraging them because users cost of retaining is only one-fifth of searching for new users. Therefore, after recognized the source of user negativeness alleviating it is first step and techniques of application recovery implement is the second step which will improve the services quality and loyalty of users.

1.11.3 Electronic word of mouth toward game applications

Volitional pre-buying communication of consumer/user is called electronic word of mouth, electronic word of mouth may take the form as like users review about application, suggestions, and opinion. As games popularity increased, game users review and eWOM of users can manipulate game demand, a number of game users, and regular communication. Positive reviews show user positiveness with the applications; positive review by the user will not only create the quality of electronic word of mouth but also will serve for increasing gaming users. Negative electronic word of mouth will decrease the number of users of a game application. User's awareness can explore through reviews, and for game developers, it is necessary that they can adequately use electronic word of mouth so that they can attract users and can improve the performance of their game.

1.12 Problem Statement

There is a little information, which is given by the Google play store about the applications that are uploaded by different developers. These applications are called third-party Android applications and millions of users download these applications.

Millions of applications have been uploaded by the hundreds of thousands of developers on daily basis. The fact is that the content uploaded on play store is largely unchecked and millions of users download this content. The objective of this research is to measure and analyze the applications' content based on the attributes of the application. We have checked the frequent patterns, correlations and sentiment analysis of dataset of the applications based on the different machine learning techniques that will be beneficial for developers and users.

1.13 Research Questions

There are a number of questions that enhance on the basis of the attributes of the dataset in this research. We have checked the causal structures from datasets, associations, correlation, frequent patterns and sentiment analysis by using different machine learning techniques. Some of the research questions that we have investigated in this research are given below:

- What is the relationship between the free and paid applications with respect to a number of inAppPurchases, ratting, installs and advertisement support?
- What are the analytical measurement and visualization of users' reviews about google play store applications?
- What is the sentiment analysis of each user review on each application?
- What are the experiences of user's positive and negative behavior toward various types of games application?
- What are the natural language processing techniques with the analysis of user reviews?

1.14 Objectives

The are some specific objectives of this research as follows:

- Explore the relationship between the free and paid applications with respect to a number of inAppPurchases, ratting, installs and advertisement support?
- Find the analytical measurement and visualization of users' reviews about google play store applications?
- Explore the sentiment analysis of each user review on each application?
- Explore the experiences of user's positive and negative behavior toward various types of games application?
- Explore the natural language processing techniques with the analysis of user reviews?

1.15 Organizational Paragraph

The rest organization of this thesis is described as follow: Chapter 1 is the introduction of the A Smart Assessment Methodology to Measure and Analyze Google Play Store. In this research thesis we have 16 sections. Chapter 2 has the literature review of this research with 1 section. Chapter 3 has the methodology and data collection of this research. In this chapter we have the 9 sections. Chapter 4 have the results and discussion of this research. In this chapter we have 21 sections. Chapter 5 has a conclusion and future work of the thesis. In this chapter we have 2 sections.

2 LITERATURE REVIEW

2.1 Background Study

Dynamic and Static analysis are two major approaches used for the analysis of the application that may be benign or malware. However, the latter is used for the detection of malware in API's. In other scenarios, the application behavior can be used in dynamic analysis to analyze and detect the malware in the application. Pons and Cons are associated with both approaches used to carry out this research. For comparison of these approaches author has analyzed the twitter data to identify the malware. A large amount of dataset is from the android application mainly extracted from AndroZoo. Each application collected from AndroZoo provides information on VirusTotal; in this tool, several antivirus programs identify the malware in application to determine whether it exists or not. As for additional information about the application, the author crawled a large dataset of tweets and analyzed the patterns of benign apps and malware on Twitter. The tweets have been scrapped by the authors based on keywords that refer to GP Store app links. These links contain the corresponding application ID that makes it easier to match tweets with the application. These tweets have been analyzed by comparing patterns in benign or malware applications with the purpose of identification of those fields that are symbolic of malware behavior. The distinction between malign and benign is perceived from AndroZoo (Fan, 2019).

There are an increasing and rising number of applications in the GP shop. There will be more than 325000 software eligible for download from the GP website, according to statistical evidence. Since the products submitted to the play store are stripped of security regulations, some healthcare apps offer defective content, and is unable to reach the required level of consistency. For this report, the authors evaluated the consistency required based on the rating scale for the applications of parental nutrition (PN). The work was performed through two big smartphone platforms: the GP shop and the Apple store. The term for study recognition is "parenteral diet." The term of 'parenteral feeding' is used to describe the main study. Due to non-free use, uninstalled upgrades < 36 months, unavailability of the English or Spanish language, non-medical form I impertinent to PN, this parenteral nutrition software is removed. To run research software, mobile or tablet computers are first downloaded. The application's reliability has been assessed using MARS (score 0:5 points). In the study of requirements, MARS utilizes a four-point analytical evaluation. Certain factors evaluated include the social score of Android users, costs, smartphones and the variety of operating systems. In the Google Drive chart, the review and data collection are done. Out of 34 requests only six proposals fulfill the requirements for exclusion and inclusion. The average social performance was 4.65. Mean MARS 2.82 (2.41-3.75) was included. The third best-known program was ASPEN eBooks (3.75): Diet Parenteral UCI (2.68). Subjective evaluation (2.5, 3.25 and 2.25, respectively) was also gained from these tests. The other programs evaluated provided a discretionary rating of < 2 and a MARS <3 (Rorís et al., 2016).

Developers aim for fresh momentum thanks to the popularity of the IoS device. For the performance of the application in a competitive environment, preparation is important. The device may be tested for success by means of the proxy. The problem emerges here: what are the metric variables that decide the application 's success and unpopularity? GP Store and GitHub are also busy and provide data that can be made public; this data can be used to correlate code with the application's popularity. This research paper explores the social and technological features of an open source framework that is collected from two sources that are important to the success of apps. Authors find that the technological as well as social influences of the application's popularity was less successful compared with the typical consumer rating to describe the applications' popularity. Interestingly with GitHub, the writer contrasted the importance of social factors to technological factors (Businge et al., 2019).

A series of policies have been developed by Google for the regulation of the app developers as well as to ensure the trust and quality of the application in the app market. Application is removed from the GP store periodically, on account of infringement of policy. For instance, low-quality applications infected with malware. In fact, during two years from 2015 to 2017, almost half of the applications have been removed or replaced from the GP store, and these applications are much more than the authors expected. However, there is no study on the characterization of these removed applications despite the major number of removal of applications. In this paper firstly, the author brings to light the underlying reason behind the removal of the applications from the play store and subsequently observes the benefits for both the developers and maintainers of the market for the development of the better application ecosystem. After crawling data from GP store, authors have thoroughly investigated the various aspects that caused the removal of 790k applications from the has the GP store. For understanding the opinion polarity on social media, the semantic analysis by consumer behaviors are increasing day by day. From the user's reviews in China, there is little intention required for the development of deep learning. This paper checks the impact of deep learning from GP store users in China. By using the technique of web mining author collected, the 196,651 reviews from the GP store. The author used different approaches for semantic analysis in deep learning: support vector machine (SVM), Naïve Bayes (NB), Long Short-Term Memory (LSTM). Extracted results from these models and compared them. The author of the paper has used different models for the analysis purposes and concluded that the deep learning models have more accuracy as compared to other machine learning models. The deductions have confirmed that semantic analysis is perfect for deep learning models. Firstly, the non-average sampling data was compared with the average sampling data, at the end of the day, author ensures that non-averaging sampling data is perfect on deep learning model. Secondly, semantic analysis dictionary named as iSGoPaSD was created. Moreover, it was found that that semantic analysis in deep learning improves GP store prediction.

The present paper proposes a hybrid sensor network model for the simple protection and wellness monitoring program related to the web of matters (IoT). The computer is built to improve the external office security (Williams et al., 2019). The suggested interface involves a portable WBAN device to access user details and an LPWAN program to integrate WBAN for the internet Web (Santa et al., 2019). The WBAN network framework is still accessible. WWAN detectors are used to determine the environmental requirements of a risk-free node in the region and to monitor the most important signals of niche for an overall node of safety. A specific group monitor, who addresses the raw detector signals, shows physiological and ambient details and often triggers a alert when an inattentive emergency scenario is detected, is inserted into the expected network. A IoT platform server has been used to include wider transmissions, such as network monitoring or cellular usage (Srinivas, 2019), in order to access the portal with a regional Web site.

Online Objects (IoT), a modern concept has now evolved, connecting a broad variety of physical and virtual items with sensors, detectors, actuators and applications that effectively access and share knowledge. Throughout general and in particular regions including mental wellbeing, IoT is gradually focused on the big study issue from the medical industry. The key purpose of this paper will be to provide an summary of recent work in the area of literature, "in which IoT primary technologies and mental health programs are covered. Google Scholar,' IEEE Xplore, Medline, Scientific Immediate and Web of Knowledge, despite the reality that the preceding ten decades, from 2008 on, were the repositories used to carry out the review (Owens et al., 2019).

Many study criteria such as "IoT or Web Objects and Mental Health" were developed, which presumably dictated the very interesting material. There are a total of 51 articles on IoT-based apps and mental health resources, 14 of which are identified as key roles of emotional well-being. A variety of (more than 60%) books used to demonstrate the program designed to monitor emotional illness individuals through detectors and integrated devices. In addition to the improved well-being of this completely new IoT development breakthrough, the detection of fertility and the delivery of alarm and advice are gaining. In disorders such as mental wellbeing, the overall quality of person lives and the productivity of their health services are often important (Havaei et al., 2019).

Throughout this paper, writers suggest a general system for designing applications throughout app stores to process, summarize and interpret consumer feedback. Our system dynamically collects specific features from user feedback, e.g. configuration details, glitches, and specifications in order to evaluate the feeling of each. Our architecture has three key elements, namely, I simulation of subjects, (ii) study of emotion and (iii) description gui. The simulation block attempts to locate semantine themes from textual commentaries that derive the goal features based on the most important words of each term. A sensation analysis block senses the sensation of each element found (Di Sorbo et al., 2016). The overview design helps users to intuitively display the apps (i.e., topics) along with their corresponding feeling, and offers detailed details rather than a 'star ranking' approach. Our evaluation demonstrates that the topic modeling framework may organise knowledge that is subcategorized by the users so that it recognizes characteristics which could have a positive / negative impact on the general evaluation of the program. With regard to happiness of the customer, authors will find that while the star rating is a reasonable measure of appraisal, it is more accurate to catch the user's feeling with a comment (Maalej and Nabil, 2015).

Authors present AUREA, a revolutionary application that automatically classifies, scans and analyzes mobile device ratings using fine seed web topics. Authors are dedicated to helping users obtain relevant and useful input from their comments in order to prepare their projects in terms of maintenance and development activities. Tests are also challenging to interpret since the document is unstructured and its length, so about a third of them are insightful. Authors claim that the developers can save a lot of time by utilizing our platform in order to evaluate and appreciate the challenges that users face (Ciurumelea et al., 2018).

Sentity analysis of user ratings was addressed by the scientists. The author plans to address in this analysis the motorized solution that works for the developers. Users can capture, search, and analyze customer ratings using the methodology. They use clear language approaches to identify aspects of the fine-grained device in comments. The consumer provides an appraisal of known functionality by presenting all feedback with a-pitch in this extract (Al-Subaihin et al., 2015). Authors can combine fine grained features into smoother and more concrete characteristics by utilizing thematic mapping techniques. We contrasted the findings of the 7 apps taken from the Apple and Google play store. Their study was done by peers. It helps the software developer to regularly analyze the user 's viewpoint on a particular, impertinent function and filter view. You have the accuracy up to 91% and recall up to 73%. The deduction implies that the summaries provided are compatible and that features have been listed in the examinations (Panichella et al., 2016).

Today, with the fervent enthusiasm for new technology, the usage of applications has growing. Consumers choose smartphones with both forms of internet devices. In fact , people have already downloaded smartphone apps based on who has previously downloaded and updated the application (Puram and Singh, 2018). False ranking points in the mobile app market that lead to mobile apps being added to the popularity list. Of note, the usage of bogus process is more commonly employed by web developers. The paper suggests the semanthropic study of the fraud detecting software for smartphone phones. The writers first suggested that the misrepresentation be better identified by excavating the active times of mobile devices, often named leading sessions (Wang et al., 2019). Authors often plan to study and utilize Natural Language (NLP) analysis in classification to obtain action verbs. Several forms of facts are included in the NLP. Instead, authors decided to translate study to reviews and eventually carry out session trend analysis of user data from the app store. The paper suggested a way of validating the usefulness of the detection algorithm and showing the scalability of it (Puram and Singh).

For this article, writers have created a managerial and organic manure (MoAPOM) Android-based framework. The MoAPOM technology primarily targets small and medium-sized farmers who want to boost crop productivity MoAPOM was developed to turn the conventional organic manure processing process using a human to person interface and the intelligent robot help device into a human contact tool. Five versions of fertilizer, organic and earthworm compost, green manure, livestock, cow dung and kitchen waste, are generated in the development phase. This program is used for communicating portability and easy GUI, ease of installation, timeliness, multiple tutorials and offline use since the MoAPOM framework has been verified for offline (Arogundade et al., 2019).

The IoT apps (the Internet of Things) produce a huge part of data and contribute to cloud storage. Such details was used to determine supply specifications for seeds, economies, crop production and specifications for fertilizers. The forecast can then be done and achieved with a smartphone application against the farmer, based on various data mining techniques. The purpose of this proposal is to increase the agriculture and seed output costs more beneficial for farmers (Ruan et al., 2019).

In order to manage large and dynamic data collection, the sensing program will develop programming skills. IoT supplies computers for both knowledge and retrieval. Cloud storage offers IoT applications with software and tools to outsource the research and processing. A unique potential is created for the growth and progress of an IoT-based framework. The creation of an architecture and collaboration model is part of this research project to allow use of the computing tools accessible. The platform has a modern network architecture, which incorporates mobile Clude Computing (MCC) paradigm with computing capability and sensing. The investigators have demonstrated via the analysis that this technology can be found in different real-life applications. The software is versatile and can achieve more complicated functions.

App obfuscation is suggested for defense against often repackaged or plagiarized Android apps. There is also little evidence accessible for developers for total device interference. This paper analyzes the authors' interpretation of the problems raised by

Android device obscuration. In this paper, analysts have examined 1.7 million applications and note that 24.92% of apps have been hidden by developers in terms of performance (Wermke et al., 2018). 308 Google play store developers have reviewed their interactions with obscurantism to grasp the definition and intention of obfuscation readers. After examining developers' knowledge, the writers conclude why developers are afraid of plagiarizing their application, so that their application may be challenged. Authors provide a follow-up analysis in which 70 respondents did not confuse a practical research program and all of the researchers falsely conclude that it was a positive. Further work is needed to render the method of obfuscation further available. Their IP was stolen, their applications repackaged and released as ransomware, and to boost the safety of the whole Android ecosystem in order to warn users about the danger that their devices would reverse engineered (Deo et al., 2016).

The semantine study focused on customer attitudes was increased everyday to obtain an appreciation of the perception polarity of social media. In China, there is no ambition to build deep learning centered on consumer feedback. This paper explores the effect on Google Play Store consumers in China of deep learning. The 196,651 comments in the Google Play Store, utilizing the web mining technique obtained. Specific methods for semanthropic computing are used by SVM (Cherkassky and Ma, 2004), Naïve Bayes (NB) (Chen et al., 2009), Long Short Memory and Deep Learning (LSTM) (Hochreiter and Schmidhuber, 1997). Obtaining and analyzing the effects of these simulations. Upon research , investigators evaluated the deep learning models were used in this paper type study rather than the precision of all other models. The findings of authors have shown that conceptual deep learning research on the profound thinking paradigm is fine. The first argument is to insure that the non-random sampling data is better in the deep learning model relative to the normal sampling data. Secondly, create the semanticized dictionary known as iSGoPaSD. Fourth of all, it indicates that semantic modeling boosts Google's estimation of plays in deep learning (Day and Lin, 2017).

The application collection method should be effective and scalable. These systems are too late, too, because authors find that today's screening mechanism is less able to detect emerging challenges. In this post, the writers discuss the applications that are created and propagated in the market by using malware from Android. These programs are just a repackaging of the same deceptive material as legitimate programs. Such implementations are also characterized by the same repackaging roots. Such programs can not always be interlinked. In this research investigators use a technique named MassVet to pick the program on a wide scale without being aware of vulnerabilities in applications (Zhang et al., 2014). This technique is used in this study. The key theme of this research is to clearly identify applications which just repackage certain apps that are already on the market, as well as applications that use the same original user interface. MassVet is based on a stream processing system and even tests the 1.3 million requirements from 33 applications worldwide. In 10 seconds writers will identify the program with the very small false error rate by utilizing this technique. The VirusTotal scanner like McAfee, NOD32 is also done through this technique. In spite of the virus identification scope, this tool operates with millions of harmful uses (Chen et al., 2015).

A million apps are submitted by the users on a regular basis. Millions of people access these software without a double-check. In fact, some information is given regarding such applications in a play store. In this report, authors focus on developing a PlayDrone rawler, the first customizable rawler to scrape millions of Google Play Store applications regular (Lindorfer et al., 2014). PlayDrone uses different methods of hacking and cracking to avoid Google filtering of games in Google's play store. Furthermore, the source code of the 880,000 program, free of charge, is open (Viennot et al., 2014).

Reviews can be a good source of knowledge for engineers' requirements. In recent years , various methods have been planned for the classification of user feedback as bug reports. Engineers are not allowed to search at the opinion and mood of consumers with respect to the particular element of concern for any method taken in these modern methods. The architecture specifications may be helpfully assisted by the presence of apps for evaluating those roles during priority setting and elicitation behavior. This thesis provides a overview of the tool-supported approach taken as regards the basic features of specifications for engineering decisions. The app that has been chosen by the interface system would require us (i) to locate product comments, (ii) to recognize bug issues, to fix queries, and user reactions to this function and (iii) to provide feedbacks to users on all apps in a dashboard. The analysis input in three-fold I analysis defined a new challenge for the consumer to look at a product, (ii) the second study offers a technical overview of a method for analytics that solves the issue, and the third study discusses the preliminary findings of search elements of the method.

The value of smartphone devices and streaming channels has moved beyond fixed links to the internet. At the same time , consumers can check for, pay for, and update smartphone applications in app stores and offer input on devices through ratings and pricing. Any analysis of the software will include user feedback and opinions on the product, functionality suggestions and bug reports. That is why testing is important to both consumers, developers and tech businesses as customers are involved in reviews, because they want to enhance the functionality of the product with the time needed, what other users say of this program, developers and software firms. A steady rise in the amount of smartphone apps and web stores contributes to improved sales for web retailers, data processing and studies in opinion gathering. App production companies and app stores authorities must ask for fair and accurate views on the study value in the worlds of applications and consumers testing comparatively recent devices for business analysis and marketing purposes. In addition, a range of studies track web consumer items, and studies concentrate mainly on smartphone device stores and user feedback are also available. Good-based literature review seeks to provide an agreed potential remedy for online mining views in app store consumer feedback, frustration and unresolved domain problem, to provide additional technical requirements, product creation and advice for more study.

New knowledge sharing entries have been released on the Site. The growth of internet existence has slowly grown, allowing extraordinary doors available for indigenous people to openly share their opinion. But the analysis of such emotions has real bottlenecks. Feeling research contributes to optimizing consumer service through a customized gui, organisation or system. Around that stage the learning algorithm must decide which emotions are influenced by observable knowledge. Assume that in social networks one thing the machine can do is render something that lighten atmosphere and alter ties, like the background color progressively noticeable if someone is tired and depressed. The platform immediately takes a step to recommend connections with users and apps to enhance the state of mind. The summary on feelings analysis, including introduction of feelings analysis, previous experience of feelings analysis, emotion analysis, statistical methods. The nostalgic research project is meant to upgrade the individuals inside the corporate network environment, as well as the systems and frameworks' implementations, thus increasing the context and the history of the system. Explore the study of android device ratings and their characteristics. We use analysis of two new programs, one of brain and puzzle and another of type configuration. 600 comments were received. In research summarization, the SAS Enterprise Miner TM 7.1 is used and the SAS 12.1 in emotion analysis. They use rules-based structures to check datasets afterwards. For widget implementations the outcome indicates 86% accuracy to the positive directory and 94% accuracy to the negative directory. 2) 94% in positive and 90% in negative for software applications. We therefore suggest that the rule-based approach is a more accurate and efficient method to conduct analyzes after contrasting the mathematical model and the rule-based model. Think of the study of emotions and extraction of thought. They discuss different issues in the group. Their primary focus is 'sensation and problems study.' It follows that the information system has a broad variety of applications and its classification is based on the domain or subject. We then suggest that no classification model is performance reliable, and that various styles of classification algorithms are efficiently merged to solve individual problems and benefit from the benefits of each other and eventually improve the ranking efficiency of the feelings.

Describes a remote sensing Random Forest Classifier. This analysis demonstrates the efficiency relation of vector support machines with random forest classification. The research was carried out in seven separate parts of the United Kingdom. This reveals that the random classification for forests is just as performing in terms of precision to help vector machines. This study suggests that it is simpler to identify random forests when less parameters are required. It is the most accurate approach too. Many capabilities include the ability to address issues including inconsistent data and loss of values. The fact that numerous features are fairly relevant throughout the process of classification is its unique aspect. The measurement of similarity also offers a means to spot outliers. Work is still underway to test random forestry classification results.

The analytical research explains the naive description of the Bayes. Despite its inaccuracies and likelihood projections, this model is proven effective in practice. For fully grasp the data features, this approach must be updated. The purpose of this analysis is to understand the working of the data characteristics. To this end, the author used Montevallo simulations which allow randomly created problems to be studied systematically. It analyzes the effect on the classification error of distribution entropy. In case of fully isolated apps or dynamically dependent elements, Naive Bayes performs well, with the poorest results between its two extremes. The preciosity is determined by shared class specifications. The lack of knowledge regarding the Naive Bayes model is a strong measure of its accuracy.

A great many smartphone apps are now downloaded and used worldwide. Android apps are sold through various device stores, such as Google Play, Apple App Store, Windows Phone Marketplace, etc. The heterogeneity of mobile applications, including Android, Apple iOS, and Windows, is perhaps one of the most interesting challenges of mobile device growth. Not too long-ago businesses like Microsoft, Adobe and a growing network of creators of integrated applications looked like a potential response to the proliferation of smartphone platforms. Hybrid mobile applications for websites are continuous and web-based (Mellish and Sun, 2005). The writers offer an analytical overview of smartphone hybrid devices in this article. The aim is also to define and analyze the capacity and differentiation of hybrid technologies delivered publicly from the viewpoint of consumers. The research was carried out with sampling 11,917 free software and 3,041,315 ratings from the Google Play Store. The result of the study establishes an entity and a reproducible description of how "from the great free" hybrid mobile creation is performed in true evaluations, thus offering a framework for potential procedures and methods for hybrid applications (Schütte et al., 2015, Yu et al., 2008).

An integral aspect of free smartphone device markets such as Google Play Store is a customer analysis. How do we integrate endless consumer feedback automatically and make sense of them? Sadly, few analytical tools can be given in user feedback in addition to basic summaries such as user ratings histograms (Liu and Zhang, 2018). The writers of this paper suggest a Wiscoma method that will evaluate hundreds of thousands of consumers in nearly three separate heights with views from smartphone software markets. Authors also indicated that their program (a) can spot anomalies in reviewal systems. (b) identify reasons why consumers hate or equally despise an item (Gomez, 2016). They can have an immersive, zooming insight on the consumer review that has developed over time. Applications of the optimized program was posted to Google Play Store's 32 GB dataset with more than 13 million consumers testing 171.493 applications for Android. The author explores how this framework will assist the business provider for smartphone apps, such as end-users, individual software developers and Google (Gómez et al., 2015, Georgiev and Georgiev, 2018).

Today, with the increasing craze in the direction of mobile devices, applications are increased. End consumers use mobile apps to access different forms of the smartphone app. This software has been downloaded based on the amount of users actually (Xu et al., 2012). Where are the comments and assessments? What'd be observations? Web apps are accessed by consumers. The product's fraud rating is an unauthorized operation in the market for smartphone apps that is included in the company's web device chart of success. This false method is used frequently by the application developer for numerous applications (Milosevic et al., 2017).

In this post, the author intends to use the client feedback for the answer to the identification of the false and scam program. Secondly, analysts diagnose an application's misrepresentation by disrupting successful time intervals, often known as leading mobile device sessions. Furthermore, the writers examine the forms of proof that updates and evaluations are focused on and that action terms are used for the purposes of natural language processing (NLP). Finally, transform comments to a session with client data obtained by the app store and conduct sample research. Therefore, the approach presented reveals the scalability and efficacy of the detection algorithm (Jha and Mahmoud, 2017a).

Over the last few decades, work has focused on mining ratings over smartphone phone stores. The bulk of the approaches introduced include improving the meta definition in user comments with various forms in insightful product criteria and uninformative recommendations. High-dimensional differences are often dictated by the basic characteristics of feedback. It increases the difficulty of the classifier may often contribute to unnecessary problems. The writers recommend the deployment of applications for review (Atkinson et al., 2008). The technique suggested concentrates on the idea of the semantic feature labeling or the lexical value of the written document in relation to semantic frames. Semantic frameworks generalize theoretical situations (contexts) from the written text. This reduces the dimensionality of the data and enriches this classifier 's overall statistical capability. Three databases are used to conduct their theoretical research for reading app feedback. The findings show, in contrast with text classification approaches, that textual frames can be used to produce lower and substantially more reliable copies. A recruitment tool for publishing of user reports to convey specific criteria. With the new protocol, a much improved sorting method is feasible and the overfitting risk is lowered (Jha and Mahmoud, 2017b).

Despite the significant health advantages of physical exercise, a considerable percentage of these people does not meet with the health tips. Thus, robust and extensively available interventions to boost degrees of physical activity are all expected. Within the last few decades, the amount of well-being insurance and physical fitness applications has steadily increased. They may shape a portion of this remedy into this widespread physical inactivity. However, it continuously unclears to that extent they use the chances of technology and sort authentic e-coaching techniques. That analysis intends to investigate the present landscape of smartphone apps that encourage physical exercise to healthy adults. For that reason, authors provide a frame to speed the degree to which this sort of apps incorporates technical capabilities (Araque et al., 2019). Authors reveal the physiological actions advertising apps included from the inspection employed a mean of about 6 functions and techniques. The capabilities which have been implemented often were user-friendly input signal, textual/numerical overviews of their consumer's behavior and advancement, sharing accomplishments or workouts in societal websites, and necessary information regarding the physical task (Liao et al., 2019). The capabilities which have been often ended up an adaptation. So, integration together with outside resources, and reinforcement using gamification, some punishment along with the option to get in touch with a specialist. The outcomes imply that apps might be made better significantly in provisions and conditions of these use of their chances that modern mobile technology offers (Groenewegen et al., 2012).

Law enforcement agents should be able to grasp the nature of the inter-connections between the criminals to understand and determine the modus operandi of an illicit operation. We studied community detection in criminal networks using the graph theory and formally introduced an algorithm that opens a new perspective of community detection. The method allows law enforcement agencies to compare the detected communities and thereby be able to assume a different viewpoint of the criminal network. We consider this method as an alternative or an addition to the traditional community detection methods mentioned earlier. The proposed algorithm allows, and will assists in the detection of different patterns and structures of the same community (Sangkaran et al., 2020a).

The study focuses on the artificial intelligence empowered road vehicle- train collision risk prediction assessment. The collision risk has been predicted to be 3.52 times higher and 77% lower in one direction. The risk is 2.95 times higher in other directions. The study predicts to reduce the road car-train collision risk to 85% at the railway level crossings. It could lead to the development of a collision avoidance system for unmanned railway level crossing (Singhal et al., 2020).

Feature engineering is used to create and optimize air quality and health features. Using residence address or any location becomes a spatial problem when the Air Quality Monitoring (AQM) stations are concentrated in urban areas. In this study, we propose a four-part spatial feature engineering algorithm to find the coordinates for health data and calculate distances with AQM stations. The algorithm will associate health records to the nearest AQM station to help reduce air pollution. The proposed algorithm is applied as a case study in Klang Valley, Malaysia. The results show that the proposed algorithm can generate air pollution health dataset efficiently (Usmani et al., 2020).

Ransomware encrypts victim's files or locks users out of the system. Petya targets individuals and companies through email attachments and download links. NotPetya has worm-like capabilities and exploits EternalBlue and EternalRomance vulnerabilities. Three-Level Security is a solution to ransomware that utilizes virtual machines along with browser extensions to perform a scan, on any files that the user wishes to download from the Internet (Ren et al., 2020).

Criminal networks analysis has attracted several numbers of researchers as network analysis gained its popularity. In this study, we have presented a comprehensive review of community detection methods based on graph analysis. More research is necessary and expected in order to further grow this research area, says the study. The concept of community was vividly discussed as well as the algorithms for detecting communities within a network (Sangkaran et al., 2020b).

The software as audit module application in IT complaint is in review in this commentary. The target of this study is to evaluate the statistical significance in relationship between client reporting attitude and client reliability. It also aims to measure the statistically noteworthy effect of client grievance conduct on service quality, and to test the impact of service quality on client dedication (Saeed et al., 2020a).

The authors are researching the use of information mining techniques to measure maximum temperature, precipitation, dissipation, and wind speed. This was done using vector help profiles, decision tree, and weather data obtained in Pakistan in 2015 and 2019. The results show that with sufficient information on cases, data mining strategies can be used to estimate the climate and environmental change that it focuses on (Saeed et al., 2020b).

Internet of Things (IoT) is revolutionizing various sectors like healthcare, military, business and more. However, this advanced technology has also caused critical security issues simultaneously. IoT networks are continuing to grow vulnerable to security attacks due to exponential connectivity of 'things' with each other. It has become crucial to address the issue of insecure routing in these IoT devices. No detection nor mitigation method has been found which addresses rank and wormhole attacks when they are initiated at the same time on an IoT network. This research aims to contribute toward design and development of high-performing and effective solutions (Jhanjhi et al., 2019).

Ransomware is made with the objective of extorting a ransom from its victim. Successful detection at this stage is crucial to enable the attack to be stopped from achieving its objective. Machine learning is proposed to detect crypto-ransomware before it starts its encryption function. This approach was used to ensure the most comprehensive detection of both known and unknown crypto- ransomware. But it may have a high false positive rate (FPR) due to the use of a pre-encryption detection algorithm (PEDA) that consists of two phases. In PEDA-Phase-I, a Windows application programming interface (API) generated by a suspicious program would be captured and analyzed. PEDA generated a signature of the suspicious program, and stored it in the signature repository, which was in Phase-II. The two phases in PEDA formed two layers of early detection for crypto-ransomware to ensure zero files lost to the user. This method can only detect known crypto- ransomware, and although very rigid, it was accurate and fast. The LA had the lowest FPR of 1.56% compared to Naive Bayes, Random Forest, Ensemble and EldeRan (Kok et al., 2019).

Data mining technology recently focuses on the methods of classification of the decision tree in data mining. The researcher use data sets for different age groups are divided into gender-related treatment for lung cancer using various modes of treatment. The age group is in between (30- 60 years) with categories in males and females. The Rattle R and Weka tools predict each group for best treatment method by which the appropriate treatment method can be analyzed. 200 real data sets were then compared in terms of the accuracy of the classification between the two different algorithms of the decision tree (Saeed et al., 2019).

3   METHODOLOGY AND DATA COLLECTION

3.1   Methodology for Analytical measurement and visualization of the Google play store content

Application on GP Store are ubiquitous. They have been classified into different categories of video, music, education, movies, games so on and so forth. The distribution has been made on the basis of the kind of content they share. Succinctly, there are two major types of applications: "free" and "paid". In this paper, a GP store dataset is populated with the sub-categories of games by using the Google-play-scraper. We scraped at least 550 applications of both free and paid type applications if these are available in sub-category. In the statistical information, we have a dataset of 10k applications of free and 3600 of paid type from all categories of games known as 'Adventure', 'Arcade', 'Action', 'Board', 'Casino', 'Casual', 'Card', 'Educational', 'Music', 'Puzzle', 'Racing', Role_Playing, Sports, 'Strategy, Simulation', 'Trivia', 'Word'. We scraped 70 different attributes of each application, however, we used four attributes for analysis in this research namely: Ratings, IAP, Advertisements support, and Installs. Sample shot of the dataset has been shown in Figure 1.

	ratings	installs	offersIAP	adSupported
1				
2	1114	100,000+	FALSE	TRUE
3	2735281	100,000,000+	TRUE	TRUE
4	249269	10,000,000+	TRUE	TRUE
5	1430466	50,000,000+	TRUE	TRUE
6	7167674	100,000,000+	TRUE	FALSE
7	8471286	100,000,000+	TRUE	TRUE
8	5428362	100,000,000+	TRUE	TRUE
9	519031	10,000,000+	TRUE	FALSE
10	2026003	50,000,000+	TRUE	TRUE
11	4716463	50,000,000+	TRUE	TRUE
12	292717	10,000,000+	TRUE	FALSE
13	7099	1,000,000+	TRUE	TRUE
14	4887	500,000+	TRUE	FALSE
15	4674	500,000+	TRUE	TRUE
16	10336264	100,000,000+	TRUE	FALSE
17	98471	10,000,000+	TRUE	TRUE
18	8393568	500,000,000+	TRUE	TRUE
19	245987	10,000,000+	TRUE	TRUE
20	2828	1,000,000+	TRUE	TRUE

Figure 1 Small Sample Screenshot of Dataset

For analyzing the attributes and checking the relationship among different attributes, we used RStudio and CIRCOS tool respectively as shown in Figure 2.

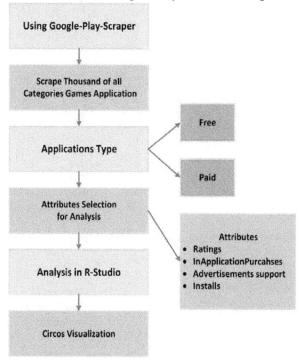

Figure 2 The Process of GP Store Analytical measurement and Dataset Visualization

3.2   Methodology for Google Play Store Use Case "Internet of Medical Things for Smart D3S to Enable Road Safety"

Any program can be located on Google Play Store. Such applications are of several different forms, such as sports, games, directions and videos. Programs are charged and optional for the two key forms. Within this article, we have created a Google Play Store Data Set of health category categories using the Google Play Scraper. Using this scraper, 550 uses of each form of health program are scraped at no expense and in the paying method. Every device in the Google Play Store has a limit of 70 apps. In this article, InAppPurcahses, Marketing Program, and Installs is named. Dataset assessment is perfomed. Data-set analysis is done in Rstudio. CIRCOS displays simulation of our research as shown in Figure 3 and Figure 4. Here title represents the name of the applications.

1	title	ratings	installs	adSupported	offersIAP
2	GoodRx Drug Prices and Coupons	72625	1,000,000+	FALSE	FALSE
3	MyChart	21345	1,000,000+	FALSE	FALSE
4	Youper - Anxiety & Depression	21088	500,000+	FALSE	FALSE
5	Anthem Anywhere	2950	500,000+	FALSE	FALSE
6	FollowMyHealthÂ®	87187	1,000,000+	FALSE	FALSE
7	Teladoc	8746	500,000+	FALSE	FALSE
8	PsyTests	15486	500,000+	FALSE	TRUE
9	OneTouch Reveal	9371	1,000,000+	FALSE	FALSE
10	Doctor On Demand	23697	1,000,000+	FALSE	FALSE
11	CVS Caremark	3996	500,000+	FALSE	FALSE
12	Pregnancy Week By Week	106532	1,000,000+	TRUE	TRUE
13	Delta Dental	1078	100,000+	FALSE	FALSE
14	BioLife Plasma Services	838	100,000+	FALSE	FALSE
15	myAirâ„¢ for Air10â„¢ by ResMed	632	100,000+	FALSE	FALSE
16	Blood Donor	4996	500,000+	FALSE	FALSE
17	Aetna Health	175	10,000+	FALSE	FALSE
18	Ovia Fertility: Ovulation & Cycle Tracker	58652	1,000,000+	FALSE	FALSE
19	KrogerRxSC	18	10,000+	FALSE	FALSE
20	Blood Pressure	35862	5,000,000+	TRUE	TRUE

Figure 3 Sample screenshot of medical applications dataset

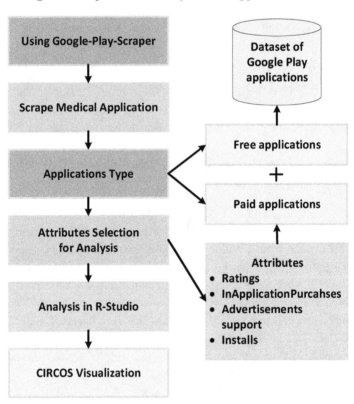

Figure 4 Methodology of Google play store Use case

3.3 Methodology for Google Play Store Use Case "Integration of Google Play Content and Frost Prediction using CNN: Events Data Collection using IoT Devices and their Detections"

Google Play Store is the central repository for the web where millions of apps have been submitted by many developers. Millions of consumers often access such apps without testing the apps' reliability and duplicity. It creates customer failure because of consumer trust harm to the Google Play Shop. In addition, there is a limited amount of knowledge regarding these applications supported by Google Play Store. We have a Google Play Store server and a Google Play Scraper for free and paying agriculture apps. By using this scraper, the top 550 applications of each agricultural form are selected in a free and paying group of operation. That Google Play Store application has 70 rating tools, including InAppPurcahses, addSupported and the amount of downloads. Example agriculture technology server screenshot is displayed in Figure 5. The findings of the study indicate the installations and scores of free and paid applications in the form of histograms, the purchasing price of such free and paid applications and the buying cost of the applications providing a proportion of the marketing subsidy for all types of agricultural use as shown in Figure 6.

	title	installs	ratings	offersIAP	adSupported
1	title	installs	ratings	offersIAP	adSupported
2	Agriculture Student(BSC Agri Notes)AGRILEARNER	50,000+	595	FALSE	TRUE
3	Agricultural Business	100,000+	523	FALSE	TRUE
4	Agriculture Dictionary	100,000+	1126	FALSE	TRUE
5	agriculture for all	5,000+	17	FALSE	TRUE
6	Agriculture quiz	50,000+	208	FALSE	TRUE
7	Agriculture Engineering	1,000+	7	FALSE	TRUE
8	Agri Zone : All in one Agri App	10,000+	349	FALSE	TRUE
9	IFFCO Kisan- Agriculture App	500,000+	3159	FALSE	FALSE
10	Real Tractor Farming Simulator 2018	1,000,000+	4015	TRUE	TRUE
11	Agricultural Business App V3.0	5,000+	9	FALSE	TRUE
12	Agriculture Engineering 101	1,000+	29	TRUE	FALSE
13	Learn Agriculture by Pictures - 1000 Images	5,000+	101	FALSE	FALSE
14	Agronote - Farm Record	10,000+	137	TRUE	TRUE
15	Agriculture News Network	10,000+	79	FALSE	TRUE
16	Agri Book	50,000+	124	FALSE	TRUE
17	Agriculture quiz	1,000+	4	FALSE	TRUE
18	Farmersgrid - Agriculture & Farming	1,000+	35	FALSE	FALSE
19	Agriculture Students,Agri notes,Agri Books	1,000+	4	FALSE	TRUE
20	Grade 12 Agricultural Sciences Mobile Application	5,000+	44	FALSE	TRUE

Figure 5 Sample screenshot of agricultural applications dataset

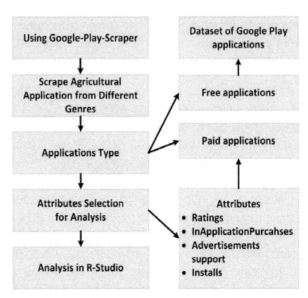

Figure 6 The methodology adopted for Google play store use case

3.4 Methodology for Experiences of user's positive and negative behavior toward various types of games application

3.4.1 Hypothesis Development

Expectation disconfirmation model explains about an individual's process of cognitive, user's behavior s positive and negative can be measured by evaluating expectations of the user about game applications with a combination of actual awareness about applications which user have. Users will always satisfy with game applications if the quality of applications meet up or exceed with user' expectations, in case of failure of match user will be dissatisfied. Absence of some necessary features during playing game process on Android applications of the user will create negativeness, but at the same time presence of this specific feature alone is not sufficient for generating positiveness higher level just because user expected from these features and not much satisfied due to lack of ability to generate high-level positiveness. On the base of the preceding discussion, the research is proposing the following proposal:

3.4.2 Hypothesis 1

The positive factors and negative perceptions of the consumer against the particular category of game are not identical with each form of game. The importance of will determinant for the positive and negative mindset of the customer can be different. The multi-attribute hypothesis stressed the disparity in the estimation of the attributes of the positivity of the individual.

Model is following

$$A_O = \sum_{i=1}^{n} B_i a_i \qquad (1)$$

Here Ao is the mindset, Bi is the force of confidence in o and ai is the calculation of the extent of positivity with o and n is the amount of beliefs. The net positive interest is therefore demonstrated by the aggregated importance of an object (i.e. a good or a service) and the appraisal of that element. The model will handle various important types of game characteristics that contribute to positive and negative actions of the player. Though different factors manipulate user's opinion and attitude about play gaming applications, the degree of manipulation may differ from person to person. A game developer can highly manipulate user's attitude as compare to incidental with the help of Core behavior, services, and products which they offered. On the base of the previous discussion, the research suggested the following:

3.4.3 Hypothesis 2 (a)

In every kind of game, user's positiveness determinants toward this specific kind of game application are not equally significant.

3.4.4 Hypothesis 2 (b)

Every kind of game, user's negativeness determinants toward this specific kind of game application are not equally significant. We explain the types of the game according to the report (Trends) of the annual gaming market. We investigate four types of game applications. A large/arena games/big application/enterprise app provides a wide variety of offers and options. A mini-games/small application refers to a game that provides only some of the large/arena games/big application/enterprise app offers. Game type is a significant plan of deliberation which can manipulate the applications, procedures, offers, and target users. For example, large/arena games/big application/enterprise app offers more options as compared to mini-games/small application. Users have different opinions, prospects, and preferences according to game kinds, and all these can manipulate user's negative and positive attitude. Large/arena games/big application/enterprise app users are extra sensitively emotionally involved in their favored game. Mini-games/small application users have a little bit of devotion to the game and care more about free applications.

3.4.5 Hypothesis 3. a

The kind and significant ranking of user's positiveness determinants are dissimilar in different kind of game applications.

3.4.6 Hypothesis 3. b

The Kind and significant ranking of user's negativeness determinants is various in different kinds of the game application.

3.4.7 Data Collection

Within the new age smartphone apps are a crucial part of our lives, A study shows that between 2011 and October 2012 half a million software applications were launched. During real life citizens mainly use Ios phones; lately, Android applications are well known to all and can be used for calls, social networking, sports, browsers, and many more. Web devices provide free and paying applications; smartphone consumers may easily navigate them. Now in these days, over a million android applications are open, which are often named smartphone devices on Google Play Store. A smartphone user may pick a favorite device for a specific dataset with predefined categories from over one million mobile devices. Another important part of the data collection process is also the analysis, viability and quality of the data set. We also removed hundreds of thousands of consumers' feedback and assessments of different type software as shown in Figure 7. At the top, pick specific Google Play Store categories after selecting various Google Play Store categories. Similar scrap Every community demand. Game genres include combat, casino, sports card and gaming, analysis scraped 197,562 ratings in 5 separate types in Google Play Storage devices as shown in Table 1.

1	cetagory	app_name	app_id	reviews	rating
2	Sports	Billiards City	com.billiards.city.pool.nation.club	Wonderfull App. Completed all 1020 levels, C	5
3	Sports	Billiards City	com.billiards.city.pool.nation.club	It's good, I like the gameplay. Please change ι	4
4	Sports	Billiards City	com.billiards.city.pool.nation.club	I really enjoyed this game until I saw one of tl	1
5	Arcade	Leps World 2	at.ner.lepsWorld2	Nice	5
6	Arcade	Leps World 2	at.ner.lepsWorld2	Love it	5
7	Arcade	Leps World 2	at.ner.lepsWorld2	Good	5
8	card	Spider Solitaire	com.happysky.spider	Tons of fun and challenging to play. I really lil	5
9	card	Spider Solitaire	com.happysky.spider	Crack\u003dthis game	5
10	card	Spider Solitaire	com.happysky.spider	I love this, I end up playing for hours on end!	5
11	Sports	Snooker Stars	com.giraffegames.ggpool	Best pool game and good graphics	4
12	Sports	Snooker Stars	com.giraffegames.ggpool	Its realy good game and awsm	5
13	Sports	Snooker Stars	com.giraffegames.ggpool	Best game ever I played	5
14	Racing	Bike Mayhem Free	mobi.bestfreegames.bike.mayhem	Never played game	5
15	Racing	Bike Mayhem Free	mobi.bestfreegames.bike.mayhem	I loveeeee ittttt	5
16	Racing	Bike Mayhem Free	mobi.bestfreegames.bike.mayhem	There no ads	5

Figure 7 Sample screenshot of the dataset

Table 1 Detail description of a dataset of reviews scraped from google play store

Category of Application	Total Number of Reviews
Action	47116
Arcade	36521
Card	37761
Sports	33770
Racing	42394

3.4.8 Research Methodology

The dataset of the user reviews is in the form of the textual data. The qualitative methods are used the traditional approach in research such as content analysis and grounded theory. In the functionality of these methods, the researchers must code it subjectively and read all content as well as interpret. In this research, we have scraped the dataset of 197,562 reviews from 5 different categories of game applications from Google play store. We cannot use the traditional methods for analysis in this research; just because it is a complex process for researchers to continuous the consistency of coding schema for all 197,562 reviews. The traditional method is not a good option for analysis because of the information overload.

The work used the data mining method in this study, to address the abundance of knowledge that we have to obtain from unstructured text nontrivial, relevant and valuable details. The work has used the well-known Latent Semantic Analysis (LSA) text mining method in our study. LSA is a mathematical method that we used to gather hidden knowledge about abstract terms and phrases. Around the same time, LSA will expand on a record body's existing structure. In LSA due to its mathematical nature, we can extract summaries from user reviews, which are more objective than other approaches. We have studied in the literature that LSA has three steps for text mining procedures. For each type of game applications, we have separate spreadsheets for positive and negative user reviews. The research has used the leading data mining tool, Rapid Miner Studio in this research. The research has uploaded our dataset in Rapid Miner Studio and the process using the following steps:

We have different steps in the first step of the LSA procedure. The first step of the process is term reduction and preprocessing. Before analyzing the spreadsheet in Rapid Miner Studio, every spreadsheet will change into the document object, and a unique document ID will be assigned sequentially to each object. These documents may go by a number of preprocessing process. The very first step of the process is to change all the alphabets in the document into the lowercase form. After conversion, we have tokenized these documents with non-letter separators. The stop words which are used in the document have no useful information in reviews have to eliminate. Because the presence of these stop words in the word list is increasing the term frequency matrix, which is not necessary for the analysis. Following the stop words counting unimportant words such as "an," "a," "are," "is," "the," and "and," second step of procedure remove all those token which were in smaller amount letters such as (e.g., "s," "x,") because they have no significant information. In the third step, after the elimination of tokens ad stop words, remove those tokens and words that appeared only one document because those tokens or words have no theme. In the fourth step, we have applied a technique of term stemming on the word list. In this technique, the term stemming identified the words root and those words or tokens having the same root consider as one token. This step will decrease the dimensionality and combine the variant of the same word. The fifth step is to the identification of repeated words in the documents by applying the N-gram algorithm. After the term reduction process, we have evaluated that we have more than 1200 token in a dataset of the positive user reviews and more than 1500 token in a dataset of the negative user reviews for every kind of game application. LSA procedure's second step is the term "Term Frequency Matrix" (TF) transformation). By using the document matrix, we have converted all documents in the form of term frequency. Every cell of the document matrix maintains the information related to the occurrence of frequency for a document matrix's token. With the use of the term frequency/ inverse document frequency (TF/IDF) research have altered matrix value. This approach can reduce the weight of general terms and focus on the rare term. So instead of commonality of each document, there increase in the uniqueness of each document in results. The third stage of the LSA cycle is the special decomposition of values. The work used this approach to transform the TF/IDF matrix into the creation of three matrices, "text- by factor matrix," "single matrix meaning," and "factor matrix name." Data by factor matrix indicates that the text has a certain latent factor in its processing. The universal principles show the significance of a single element. Element matrix describes a latent element 's term loadings. The LSA evaluation findings are the same as the factor analysis. The study related each factor to high loading conditions and records for confirmation of the factor. For every result, the research has generated a spate table which has documents and high loading terms that sorted with absolute loading Then labeling the factor through analyzing the documents and high loading term concerned to a specific factor, determinate an appropriate label, interpreting the underlying area. Thus, we have analyzed all documents, high loading terms, and labeled factor with sensible meaning and according to the matching of high loading terms as shown in Figure 8.

3.5 Methodology and Data collection of Analytical Measurement and Visualization of Users' Reviews about Google Play Store Applications using Machine Learning Methods

Starting with scraping feedback of applications throughout the classification process. The feedback of the same application scrap multiple pages with score and user ranking in the Google Play Store utilizing the AppID scrap order. After scraping the raw, reviews, these reviews are in bulk, our next step of preprocessing of those reviews. In preprocessing working on different steps, normalize our reviews after this preprocessing step. These steps are removing a unique character, remove a single character, remove a single character from the start, subtracting multiple spaces with single spaces, remove prefixed, converting data into lowercase, stop words and then stemming. These are some significant steps for refining our reviews. After refining reviews, the bag of words in which a thousand of reviews collection of different application of different categories. Next phase is the implementation of the TF (Term Frequency) on feedback by means of a python code, instead TF / IDF (Term Frequency Inverse Document Frequency). Extract various features of each program after implementing TF / IDF. In the next stage Bigram, Trigram, and N-gram are based on comments utilizing a python language frequently used for knowledge recovery and text mining as shown in Figure 10. Using a separate method to distinguish naïve Bays, random forest and logistic regression using a python. Set different parameters such as precision, accuracy, recall and f1 ranking, and consider the statistical details on these parameters. Upon reviewing and evaluating study, mathematical results evaluate which algorithm has the greater precision, accuracy, recall and results score f1 and evaluate which algorithm is better fit for classification evaluation research as shown in Figure 9.

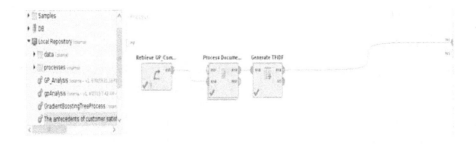

Figure 8 Methodology of Experiences of user's positive and negative behavior toward various types of games application in RapidMiner Studio

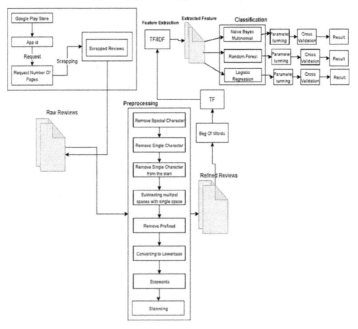

Figure 9 Classification Pipeline Diagram

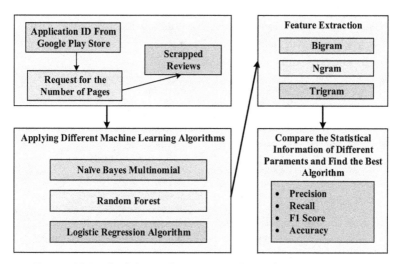

Figure 10 Methodology of reviews analysis of google play store

3.5.1 Data Collection Process

Within this analysis, hundreds of thousands of consumers analyze of test various type programs as shown in Figure 11. Pick different categories from the Google Play Store at the top. Upon choosing numerous 14 categories from the Google Play Store, each category has specific scrap framework as shown in the chart. 1. The following apps are categorized as Play, Game, Coin, Correspondence, Banking, Health and Wellness, Art, Shopping, Sports, Nature, Casual Medical and Racing Videoplay Writer. After scraping the thousands of reviews and ratings of application, must store them in a MySQL database. Convert these databases into a suitable format like .CSV file. After this is applying a preprocessing removing a unique character, remove a single character, remove a single character from the start, subtracting multiple spaces with single spaces, remove prefixed, converting data into lowercase, stop words and then stemming on this .CSV file. Then evaluating results by using a different algorithm and find the best algorithm for classification.

We have download 148 apps that appeared in 14 categories from Google play store fetch several the reviews and enter the required pages according to the reviews. There are 40 reviews on one page. Collect a total of 506259 reviews in the Google play store website, as shown in Figure 12. First, using the request library to extract the info. The request library helps the user to submit Python HTTP/1.1 queries to attach inputs such as headers, data types, multipart files and parameters using simple Python libraries. This library enables users to process python answer info. And using the re-library to process code. A regular expression is a specific sequence of characters which helps the

47

user match or identify other strings or string sets by using a specialized pattern-based syntax. Using the Lovely Soup Library by utilizing the RElibrary. Beautiful Soup software is used for HTML and XML file extraction. The library runs really well and saves time for the programmer, as shown in Table 2.

	cetagory	app_name	app_id	reviews	rating
1	cetagory	app_name	app_id	reviews	rating
2	Sports	Billiards City	com.billia	Wonderfι	5
3	Sports	Billiards City	com.billia	It's good,	4
4	Sports	Billiards City	com.billia	I really er	1
5	Sports	Billiards City	com.billia	PLEASE!!!	1
6	Sports	Billiards City	com.billia	Very easy	4
7	Sports	Athletics2: Summer	com.tangr	03e The gι	3
8	Sports	Athletics2: Summer	com.tangr	It's very n	5
9	Sports	Athletics2: Summer	com.tangr	\u003e Oκ	4
10	Sports	Athletics2: Summer	com.tangr	003c/\u00	5
11	Arcade	Bubble Shooter 2	shooter.tι	???? ?? ??	5
12	Arcade	Bubble Shooter 2	shooter.tι	Too many	1
13	Arcade	Bubble Shooter 2	shooter.tι	This game	3
14	Arcade	Bubble Shooter 2	shooter.tι	I HATE \"f	1
15	Arcade	Bubble Shooter 2	shooter.tι	Too many	1
16	Casual	Gardenscapes	com.playr	I really er	5
17	Casual	Gardenscapes	com.playr	Love all tι	5
18	Casual	Gardenscapes	com.playr	Good muι	4
19	Casual	Gardenscapes	com.playr	Love this	5
20	Casual	Gardenscapes	com.playr	The game	5

Figure 11 Sample screen short of Dataset

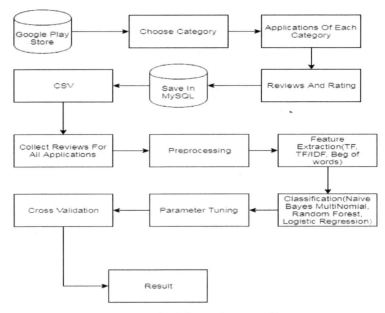

Figure 12 Methodology of Data Collection

48

Table 2 Detailed description of Dataset

Action		Arcade		Card	
App Name	**Reviews**	**App Name**	**Reviews**	**App Name**	**Reviews**
Bush Rush	4001	29 Card Game	4001	Angry Bird Rio	4481
Gun Shot Fire War	3001	Blackjack 21	1601	Bubble Shooter 2	4001
Metal Soldiers	4001	Blackjack	4481	Jewels Legend	4001
N.O.V.A Legacy	4364	Callbreak Multiplayer	4001	Lep World 2	3001
Real Gangster Crime	4001	Card Game 29	3066	Snow Bros	3001
Shadow Fight 2	4481	Card Words Kingdom	4472	Sonic Dash	4481
Sniper 3D Gun Shooter	4481	Gin Rummy	3616	Space Shooter	4401
Talking Tom Gold Run	4001	Spider Solitaire	2801	SubwayPrincesRunner	3001
Temple Run 2	3001	Teen Patti Gold	4481	Subway Surfers	4481
Warship Battle	4001	World Series of poker	4001	Super Jabber Jump 3	2912
Zombie Frontier 3	4001				
Zombie Hunter King	3782				
Communication		**Finance**		**Health and Fitness**	
App Name	**Reviews**	**App Name**	**Reviews**	**App Name**	**Reviews**
Dolphin Browser	3001	bKash	4481	Home Workout - No Equipment	4481
FireFox Browser	3001	CAIXA	1220	Home Workout for Men	1163
Google Duo	3001	CAPTETEB	697	Lose Belly Fat In 30 Days	4481
Hangout Dialer	3001	FNB Banking App	2201	Lose It! - Calorie Counter	4001
KakaoTalk	3001	Garanti Mobile Banking	859	Lose Weight Fat In 30 Days	4481
LINE	3001	Monobank	605	Nike+Run Club	1521
Messenger Talk	3001	MSN Money-Stock Quotes & News	3001	Seven - 7 Minutes Workout	4425
Opera Mini Browser	3001	Nubank	1613	Six Pack In 30 Days	3801
UC Browser Mini	3001	PhonePe-UPI Payment	4001	Water Drink Reminder	4481
WeChat	3001	QIWI Wallet	1601	YAZIO Calorie Counter	1590
		Yahoo Finance	3001		
		YapiKredi Mobile	1952		
		Stock	3001		
Photography		**Shopping**		**Sports**	
App Name	**Reviews**	**App Name**	**Reviews**	**App Name**	**Reviews**
B612 - Beauty & Filter Camera	4001	AliExpress	4481	Billiards City	4481
BeautyCam	4001	Amazon for Tablets	4481	Real Cricket 18	3001
BeautyPlus	4001	Bikroy	4481	Real Football	3001
Candy Camera	4481	Club Factory	4001	Score! Hero	3001
Google Photos	4481	Digikala	4001	Table Tennis 3D	3001
HD Camera	4001	Divar	4001	Tennis	3001
Motorola Camera	4001	Flipkart Online Shopping App	4481	Volleyball Champions 3D	3001
Music Video Maker	4001	Lazada	4481	World of Cricket	4481
Sweet Selfie	4481	Myntra Online Shopping App	4481	Pool Billiards Pro	4001
Sweet Snap	4001	Shop clues	4481	Snooker Star	2801
Video Player Editor		**Weather**		**Casual**	
App Name	**Reviews**	**App Name**	**Reviews**	**App Name**	**Reviews**

49

KIneMaster	1441	NOAA Weather Radar & Alerts	3601	Angry Bird POP	4481
Media Player	2713	The Weather Channel	4001	BLUK	3281
MX Player	3001	Transparent Weather & Clock	1441	Boards King	4481
Power Director Video Editor App	1641	Weather & Clock Weight for Android	4481	Bubble Shooter	4481
Video Player All Format	1041	Weather & Radar - Free	3601	Candy Crush Saga	4481
Video Player KM	3001	Weather Forecast	1681	Farm Heroes Super Saga	4481
Video Show	1321	Weather Live Free	1721	Hay Day	4481
VivaVideo	4190	Weather XL PRO	1401	Minion Rush	4481
You Cut App	1241	Yahoo Weather	4361	My Talking Tom	4481
YouTube	1201	Yandex. Weather	1045	Pou	4481
				Shopping Mall Girl	4481
				Gardens capes	4481

Medical		Racing	
App Name	**Reviews**	**App Name**	**Reviews**
Anatomy Learning	2401	Asphalt Nitro	4481
Diseases & Dictionary	3201	Beach Buggy Racing	4481
Disorder & Diseases Dictionary	2401	Bike Mayhem Free	4481
Drugs.com	2401	Bike Stunt Master	2745
Epocrates	1001	Dr. Driving 2	4481
Medical Image	1423	Extreme Car Driving	4481
Medical Terminology	1448	Hill Climb Racing 2	3801
Pharmapedia Pakistan	4134	Racing Fever	4481
Prognosis	2401	Racing in Car 2	4481
WikiMed	3201	Trial Xtreme 4	4481

3.6 Data collection of Android application ranking through sentiment analysis of user comments

When we know, smartphone phones are part of our lives. According to a survey, 0.675 million applications were available on the Google Play Store in 2011 and October 2012. And we gather data from the Google Play Store in this post. We receive feedback from the Google Play Store on apps. We receive 8 group ratings from Google Play Store. They evaluate various programs in every group. The ones we have shown in Table 3.

Table 3 Detailed dataset information after scrapping from Google play store

Action		Casual		Communication	
App Name	**Reviews**	**App Name**	**Reviews**	**App Name**	**Reviews**
Bush Rush	4001	Angry Bird POP	4481	Dolphin Browser	3001
Metal Soldiers	4001	Boards King	4481	Fire Fox Browser	3001
Real Gangster Crime	4001	Bubble Shooter	4481	Google Duo	3001
Talking Tom Gold Run	4001	Candy Crush Saga	4481	Hangouts Dialer	3001

50

App Name	Reviews	App Name	Reviews	App Name	Reviews
Warship Battle	4001	Farm Heroes Super Saga	4481	KakaoTalk	3001
Zombie Frontier 3	4001	Hay Day	4481	LINE	3001
		Minion Rush	4481	Messenger Lite	3001
		My Talking Tom	4481	Opera Mini Browser Beta	3001
		Pou	4481	UC Browser Mini	3001
		GardenScapes	4481	WeChat	3001
Photography		**Racing**		**Shopping**	
App Name	**Reviews**	**App Name**	**Reviews**	**App Name**	**Reviews**
B612 - Beauty & Filter Camera	4001	Asphalt Nitro	4481	AliExpress	4481
BeautyCam	4001	Beach Buggy Racing	4481	Amazon for Tablets	4481
BeautyPlus	4001	Bike Mayhem Free	4481	Bikroy	4481
HD Camera	4001	Dr. Driving 2	4481	Flipkart Online Shopping App	4481
Motorola Camera	4001	Extreme Car Driving	4481	Lazada	4481
Music Video Maker	4001	Racing Fever	4481	Myntra Online Shopping App	4481
Sweet Snap	4001	Racing in Car 2	4481	Snapdeal Online Shopping App	4481
		Trial Xtreme 4	4481	Shopclues	4481
Art & Design		**Health & Fitness**			
App Name	**Reviews**	**App Name**	**Reviews**		
Canvas	4001	Home Workout - No Equipment	4481		
ibis Paint XChanger	4001	Lose Belly Fat In 30 Days	4481		
PaperColor: Paint Draw Sketchbook & PaperDraw	4001	Lose Weight Fat In 30 Days	4481		
Sketch - Draw & Paint	4001	Water Drink Reminder	4481		

3.6.1 Methodology of Android application ranking through sentiment analysis of user comments

First, we selected Action category. Inside this we fetch top 6 applications reviews and their rating. We fetch the total 24006 reviews. At Second, we selected Casual category. Inside this we fetch top 10 applications reviews and their rating. We fetch the total 44810 reviews. At Third, we selected Communication category. We fetch top 10 applications comments and their rating. Inside it we fetch the total 30010 reviews. At forth, we selected Photography category. Inside this we fetch top 7 applications reviews and their rating. we fetch the total 28007 reviews. At fifth, we selected Racing category. Inside this we fetch top 8 applications reviews and their rating. We fetch the total 35848 reviews. At Sixth, we selected shopping category. Inside this we fetch top 8 applications reviews and their rating. We fetch the total 35848 reviews. At seventh, we selected Art & Design category. We fetch top 8 applications reviews and their rating. Inside it we fetch the total 35208 reviews. At last, we selected Health & Fitness category. Inside this we fetch top 4 applications reviews and their rating. we fetch the total 17924 reviews. We fetch number of the reviews and enter the required pages according to the comments. we collect total 251661 reviews in the Google play store as shown in Figure 13 . First of all, we used to order the library to capture the details. The library requests require the user to submit Python HTTP/1.1 queries. Using the Python repository, we incorporate material such as headers, tables, multi-part directories, and parameters. This library allows users to process python response data fairly. Additionally, we used the re database. Regular expression is a specific character sequence which enables the user to match or find other strings or string sets, using a different syntax kept in a script. We used the Beautiful Soup on the sixth. This is a python module that extracts data from HTML and XML formats. It library runs really quickly and saves time for programmers. Then we used the OS library at the end. We used to enter the domain Id and number of pages for fetching comments. Within one article there are 40 comments. We also reached the same number of pages that we have to retrieve feedback as shown in Figure 14.

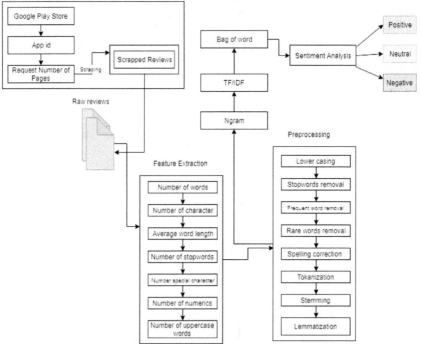

Figure 13 Methodology of sentiment analysis

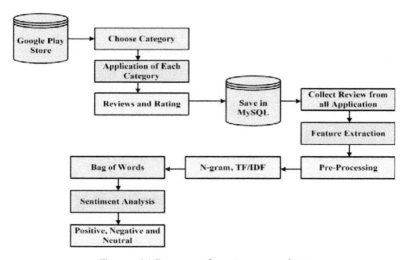

Figure 14 Process of sentiment analysis

Now when we fetch the reviews of different categories. So, we had performed some actions in this data. Some steps following:

3.7 Basic feature extraction using reviews

We use user reviews from Google play store to perform the sentiment analysis. To perform the different task in sequence let's quickly read the CSV file.

3.7.1 Number of Words

We have scraped thousands of reviews Google play store, the first step we have extracted number of words from each review of user. The basic research behind this step is that the negative reviews of user have lesser number of words as in comparison of positive reviews. The source code for finding the number of words and the sample shot of result is shown in Figure 15.

```
train['word_count'] = train['reviews'].apply(lambda x: len(str(x).split(" ")))
train[['reviews','word_count']].head()
```

	reviews	word_count
0	I cannot speak highly enough about Canva. It ...	53
1	Dear canva team, your app is working great an...	54
2	It was good, i love everything about it. the ...	63
3	Easy to use , made a invitation in less than ...	44
4	its a great app and all. i wld give 5 stars i...	54

Figure 15 Working screenshot of the number of words

53

3.7.2 Number of characters

After finding the number of words we have same thinking and calculate the number of characters in each review from user on specific application. We have done by calculating the length of review. The source code for finding the number of character and the sample shot of result is shown in Figure 16.

```
train['char_count'] = train['reviews'].str.len()
train[['reviews','char_count']].head()
```

	reviews	char_count
0	I cannot speak highly enough about Canva. It ...	298
1	Dear canva team, your app is working great an...	273
2	It was good, i love everything about it. the ...	327
3	Easy to use , made a invitation in less than ...	226
4	its a great app and all. i wld give 5 stars i...	249

Figure 16 Working screenshot of the number of characters

3.7.3 Average Word Length

We have calculated the average word length of each review in the next step. This step is more important for improving our model. In this step we have calculated the sum of words from each review and divide these words of total length of the review. The source code for finding the average word length and the sample shot of result is shown in Figure 17.

```
train['avg_word'] = train['reviews'].apply(lambda x: avg_word(x))
train[['reviews','avg_word']].head()
```

	reviews	avg_word
0	I cannot speak highly enough about Canva. It ...	4.730769
1	Dear canva team, your app is working great an...	4.150943
2	It was good, i love everything about it. the ...	4.274194
3	Easy to use , made a invitation in less than ...	4.255814
4	its a great app and all. i wld give 5 stars i...	3.698113

Figure 17 Working screenshot of average word of length

3.7.4 Number of stop words

When we are solving the natural language processing (NLP) we have removed the stop words first. The number of stop words can also calculate some extra information which we might be have lost. By using the NLTK library we have imported stop words. The source code for finding the number of stop words and the sample shot of result is shown in Figure 18.

```
from nltk.corpus import stopwords
stop = stopwords.words('english')

train['stopwords'] = train['reviews'].apply(lambda x: len([x for x in x.split() if x in stop]))
train[['reviews','stopwords']].head()
```

	reviews	stopwords
0	I cannot speak highly enough about Canva. It ...	18
1	Dear canva team, your app is working great an...	19
2	It was good, i love everything about it. the ...	31
3	Easy to use , made a invitation in less than ...	17
4	its a great app and all. i wld give 5 stars i...	23

Figure 18 Working screenshot of number of stop words

3.7.5 Number of special characters

There are different special characters are used in user reviews. In the next step we have extracted the number of hashtags or mentions and calculate them. We can also extract some more information about the reviews.

Hashtags or mentions always appear at the beginning of a word that's why we have used it with 'start function'. The source code for finding the number of special characters and the sample shot of result is shown in Figure 19.

```
train['hastags'] = train['reviews'].apply(lambda x: len([x for x in x.split() if x.startswith('#')]))
train[['reviews','hastags']].head()
```

	reviews	hastags
0	I cannot speak highly enough about Canva. It ...	0
1	Dear canva team, your app is working great an...	0
2	It was good, i love everything about it. the ...	0
3	Easy to use , made a invitation in less than ...	0
4	its a great app and all. i wld give 5 stars i...	0

Figure 19 Working screenshot of number of special characters

3.7.6 Number of numeric

We have calculated the number of numeric in user reviews just like we have calculated the number of words. That step is sometime is not in practices, but it could be more informative while doing similar exercises. The source code for finding the number of numeric and the sample shot of result is shown in Figure 20.

```
train['numerics'] = train['reviews'].apply(lambda x: len([x for x in x.split() if x.isdigit()]))
train[['reviews','numerics']].head()
```

	reviews	numerics
0	I cannot speak highly enough about Canva. It ...	0
1	Dear canva team, your app is working great an...	0
2	It was good. i love everything about it. the ...	0
3	Easy to use , made a invitation in less than ...	2
4	its a great app and all. i wld give 5 stars i...	1

Figure 20 Working screenshot of number of numeric

3.7.7 Number of Uppercase words

Sometime user expresses his feelings in the form of capital words like anger and rage are often written in UPPERCASE words. That's why thus is more important step to identify those words. The source code for finding the number of uppercase words and the sample shot of result is shown in Figure 21.

```
train['upper'] = train['reviews'].apply(lambda x: len([x for x in x.split() if x.isupper()]))
train[['reviews','upper']].head()
```

	reviews	upper
0	I cannot speak highly enough about Canva. It ...	2
1	Dear canva team, your app is working great an...	3
2	It was good. i love everything about it. the ...	0
3	Easy to use , made a invitation in less than ...	0
4	its a great app and all. i wld give 5 stars i...	0

Figure 21 Working screenshot of number of uppercase words

3.8 Basic Pre-processing

We have learned so far how basic features extraction from reviews. Before text and feature extraction, we have cleaned our dataset for obtaining the best features. We have achieved these features by doing basis pre-processing steps on training dataset.

3.8.1 Lower case

In first step we have transformed our dataset into the lower case. We can avoid the replication of same words in our dataset. For example, when we are calculating the word count the 'Analytics' and 'analytics' taken as different words. The source code for finding the lower case and the sample shot of result is shown in Figure 22.

```
train['reviews'] = train['reviews'].apply(lambda x: " ".join(x.lower() for x in x.split()))
train['reviews'].head()
```

```
0    i cannot speak highly enough about canva. it h...
1    dear canva team, your app is working great and...
2    it was good, i love everything about it. the r...
3    easy to use , made a invitation in less than 3...
4    its a great app and all. i wld give 5 stars if...
```

Figure 22 Working screenshot of lower case in basic pre-processing

3.8.2 Removal of Stop Words

We have discussed stop words removal earlier in basic feature extraction from user reviews. In basic pre-processing we have followed the same earlier routine. We have used a predefined library or either used a list of stop words. The source code for removal of stop words and the sample shot of result is shown in Figure 23.

```
from nltk.corpus import stopwords
stop = stopwords.words('english')
train['reviews'] = train['reviews'].apply(lambda x: " ".join(x for x in x.split() if x not in stop))
train['reviews'].head()

0    cannot speak highly enough canva. given tools ...
1    dear canva team, app working great love it. jo...
2    good, love everything it. reason four star ins...
3    easy use , made invitation less 30 mins apprec...
4    great app all. wld give 5 stars inapp store gr...
```

Figure 23 Working screenshot of removal of stop words in basic pre-processing

3.8.3 Common word removal

In previous step we have just removed stop words, but in this step, we have removed common words. We have collected 10 most frequent occurring words then take a call to retain or remove. We have removed those words that are not used in classification of user reviews. The source code for removal of common words and the sample shot of result is shown in Figure 24.

```
freq = list(freq.index)
train['reviews'] = train['reviews'].apply(lambda x: " ".join(x for x in x.split() if x not in freq))
train['reviews'].head()

0    cannot speak highly enough canva. given tools ...
1    dear canva team, working it. join friend's des...
2    good, everything it. reason four star instead ...
3    , made invitation less 30 mins appreciate with...
4    all. wld give 5 stars inapp store graphics che...
```

Figure 24 Working screenshot of common word removal in basic pre-processing

3.8.4 Rare words removal

In last step we have removed most common words, in next step we have removed most rare words from the user review. Due to the rareness the association between them and other words is dominated by noise. We can replace the are words with the general word form to increase the count of the words. The source code for removal of rare words and the sample shot of result is shown in Figure 25.

```
freq = list(freq.index)
train['reviews'] = train['reviews'].apply(lambda x: " ".join(x for x in x.split() if x not in freq))
train['reviews'].head()
```

```
0    cannot speak highly enough canva. given tools ...
1    dear canva team, working it. join friend's des...
2    good, everything it. reason four star instead ...
3    , made invitation less 30 mins appreciate with...
4    all. wld give 5 stars inapp store graphics che...
```

Figure 25 Working screenshot of rare word removal in basic pre-processing

3.8.5 Spelling correction

We use the "textblob" library for spelling correction because this step is more useful in pre-processing for reducing the copies of words. Also, for understanding of those words which are completely not understandable in reading. The source code for spelling correction and the sample shot of result is shown in Figure 26.

```
0    cannot speak highly enough canvas. given tools..
1    dear canvas team, working it. join friend's de..
2    good, everything it. reason four star instead ..
3    , made invitation less 30 mind appreciate with..
4    all. old give 5 stars inapt store graphics che..
```

Figure 26 Working screenshot of spelling correction in basic pre-processing

3.8.6 Tokenization

To dividing the user reviews in sequence of words or sentences we used tokenization. We have transformed user reviews into a blob and then converted them in series of word by using the "textblob" library. The source code for tokenization and the sample shot of result is shown in Figure 27.

```
'dear', 'canva', 'team', 'working', 'it', 'join', 'friend'
```

Figure 27 Working screenshot of Tokenization in basic pre-processing

3.8.7 Stemming

By using a simple rule-based approach a stemming refers to the removal of suffices, like "ing", "ly", "s" and so on. We have used PorterStemmer from the NLTK library. The source code for stemming and the sample shot of result is shown in Figure 28.

```
0    cannot speak highli enough canva. given tool c...
1    dear canva team, work it. join friend' design ...
2    good, everyth it. reason four star instead fiv...
3    , made invit less 30 min appreci without ad . ...
4    all. wld give 5 star inapp store graphic cheap...
```

Figure 28 Working screenshot of stemming in basic pre-processing

3.8.8 Lemmatization

Lemmatization converts the word into its root word, rather than just stripping the suffices. To obtain the root word lemmatization makes use of the vocabulary and does a morphological analysis. Therefore, we usually prefer using lemmatization over stemming. The source code for lemmatization and the sample shot of result is shown in Figure 29.

```
0    cannot speak highly enough canva. given tool c...
1    dear canva team, working it. join friend's des...
2    good, everything it. reason four star instead ...
3    , made invitation le 30 min appreciate without...
4    all. wld give 5 star inapp store graphic cheap...
```

Figure 29 Working screenshot of lemmatization in basic pre-processing

3.9 Advance Text Processing

we have cleaned our dataset in basic pre-processing steps, now we have to extract featured from our dataset by using a natural language processing.

3.9.1 N-grams

The combination of the multiple words together is known as N-grams. The N=1 is called unigram, respectively N=2 is bigram, N=3 is trigram. Unigram has not a maximum information as in comparison of bigram and trigram. The language structure is the basic method behind the n-gram, like what letter or word is likely to follow the given one. the more context you must work is longer n-gram. We can fail to grab the important information when the length of n-gram is too short. If the length of the string is too long than we may fail to capture the "general knowledge" and only stick to cases. The n-grams function of the "textblob" library to extract bigrams from our reviews as shown in Figure 30.

```
[WordList(['can', 'not']), WordList(['not', 'speak']),
```

Figure 30 Working screenshot of n-gram in advance text pre-processing

3.9.2 Term Frequency / Inverse Document Frequency (TF-IDF)

3.9.2.1 Term frequency

Term frequency is simply used to count the length of the sentence. We can generalize term frequency as:

TF = (Number of times term T appears in the particular row) / (number of terms in that row)

3.9.2.2 Inverse Document Frequency

That word's IDF is the log of the proportion of the total number of rows to the number of rows in the word. IDF = log (N / n), where N represents the total number of rows and n is the number of rows with the term as shown in Figure 31.

```
        words  tf       idf       tfidf
0        join   2  8.006368  16.012735
1      design   1  3.740173   3.740173
2     android   1  4.665274   4.665274
3     related   1  7.600902   7.600902
4       canva   1  3.828142   3.828142
5      shared   1  8.411833   8.411833
```

Figure 31 Working screenshot of IDF in advance text pre-processing

We can see that the TF-IDF has penalized terms such as "do not," "don't" and "use," since such terms also occur. However, it has granted "enter" a significant weight because this would be quite useful to decide the opinion of the study.

3.9.3 Bag of Words

The term appearance in the comments is referred to as Bag of Words (BOW). The primary aim of the Bag of Words (BOW) is to ensure that two identical text fields have a common word form and thus a specific word container.

3.9.4 Sentiment Analysis

The emotion analysis is determined for increasing evaluation of all applications. Growing analysis has a weight, varying from -1 to +1. In it we use the library Textblob to locate this study. Textblob is a python module for textual data analysis. Text blob executes the normal linguistic retrieval function quickly. It offers a quick API to conduct natural language tasks such as part-of-speech marking, extracting a statement, interpretation of emotions, description, translation, etc. For that we use the Naive Bayes system. It is used for grouping, requiring broad data sets for preparation. The existence of the specific function is believed to be independent of certain functions. Models and forecasts can be made easily as shown in Figure 32.

```
                      bad ....?  -0.700000
  awesome app. make beautiful art.   0.925000
               best art ever!!   1.000000
          way fantabulous. epic   0.100000
             amazing wish free   0.500000
```

Figure 32 Working screenshot of sentiment analysis in advance text pre-processing

4   RESULTS AND DISCUSSION

4.1   Analytical measurement and visualization of the Google play store content

4.1.1   Overview

Millions of users download these applications without any check of authentication and duplicity. These applications get the personal information of the users and so the innuendo that users are being surveilled might vandalize their trust in google services. Furthermore, a scant piece of information is provided to users about the detrimental and useful factors of applications, Consequently, user must download them first to determine their functionality. The Google-play-scraper has been used to scrap the data from Google play store with the game category and its sub-categories. With the aid of this scraper, 550 game applications that fall in both "paid" and "free" category are collected. Accumulatively, 10k free applications and 3600 paid applications are scrapped. The four attributes for the analysis are used, termed as "ratings", "inApplicationPurchases (IAP)", "advertisements support" and "Installs". The visualization is performed using the purchase rate for both types of applications i.e., paid and free. The percentage of advertisement support is taken as second parameter for both type of applications as well. A histogram represents the rating of the applications as a third parameter for free and paid applications. Another visualization in the form of histogram is demonstrated for the installation of free and paid applications and their related categories. The installation of applications is the fourth and last parameter. Visualization of the results in CIRCOS is presented, which is useful to check the relationship among attributes. The visualization is necessitous for game developers to confront the dilemma of deciding the type of games to be developed for the motives of achieving considerable number of downloads and it's also felicitous for game users to spot the games that are congruous with their personal preferences.

4.2   Results Analytical measurement and visualization of the Google play store content

Hundreds of apps are imported from Android developers in the GP shop. Without supervision and balancing, consumers can access such applications without testing the program whether this program is appropriate for the consumer or not. Fake or fraudulent apps may capture the user's personal data and destroy the user's confidence in GP stores. The validity of the application cannot be calculated since the developers have no detail at the front end of the program. Only the GP store has little knowledge regarding the application's source code. For this study, InAppPurchase as a proportion of supports for ads, reviews and downloads was visualized to reflect the histograms of free and paying medical apps in the GP shop. We visualized the interaction between various CIRCOS attributes.

4.2.1 A number of IAP

Applications of GP store are majorly classified into two types free and paid. "purchases attribute" of many applications provide information and help to the game application developer in which category of the market is more demanding. For visualization of this attribute use the pie3d chart. Visualize from the pie3d chart that in games the number of paid applications is more than many free applications as shown in Figure 33.

The total 2*pi drops the NAs and zeros because the pie3D scales the value in x. It will calculate the sequence for calls draw and for drawing the sectors, with the title sector also displays an empty plot. The pie3D label is placed in each sector if the labels are supplied. The sector color and label positions are must be equal to the number of values in x if numbers of labels are supplied. Also, if labels are long, then it will help to change the position and reduce the radius of the pie. For plotting the R objects, it is working as a generic function. This function used for more detail about the graphical parameter arguments. The default value will be used for a simple plot and scatter plot. Instead of this, there is several methods use in R for the plot is density objects, frames, data and functions and so on.

4.2.2 Free Games IAP

For the client purchasing a variety of games in the GP shop, cash, items etc. may be made accessible to the customer when completing a job or action that is conveniently not important for this specific program or game. Take an illustration of this by some game applications only purchase coins by credit card, fill up the survey form, see additional products or videos etc. Free apps also provide IAP, as no payment is paid by consumers of such programs when running free applications. We used Pie3D charts to represent the percentage of specified attributes. The ratio of the implementation of such games indicates that 34% of free games do not offer IAP and 66% of free games give IAP as shown in Figure 33.

4.2.3 Games in Paid category with IAP

The paying games charge money during installs and this is why such applications give their users more convenience and comfort. The percentage of IAP sales in the paying program is smaller. We can simulate the comparative statistics of paying IAP users, and Pie3D can imagine 83% of compensated IAP apps and only 17% of optional IAP apps as shown in Figure 33.

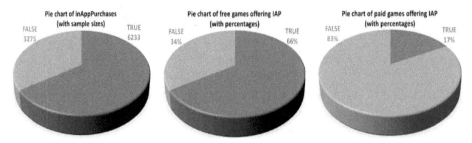

Figure 33 A Number of IAP PieChart (IAP), Free and Paid apps

4.2.4 Free Games with Advertisements Support

Advertising plays an important role in the company's success, brand, etc. In GP Store, many applications contain publicity from various companies, which sometimes frustrates users and provides helpful information. At the time of installation, this type of application doesn't take money from the user; hence the majority of the applications offer ads. The pie3d diagrams show that only 13% of free games do not offer any ads and 87% of free games offer any ads as shown in Figure 34.

4.2.5 Paid Games with Advertisements Support

The pie3D chart shows that 86% paid games do not offer advertisements and just 14% paid games to offer advertisements as shown in Figure 34. Thanks to the reality that paying programs incur those costs at deployment time. These advertisements frustrate the consumer of the program for a period, but the paying device owners maintain the client's comfort zone. The promotional level for paying software is smaller relative to free apps.

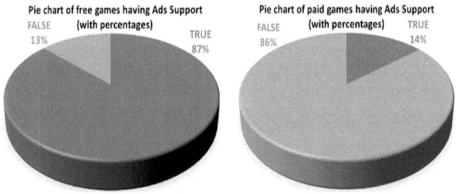

Figure 34 Distribution of free and paid games apps with advertisements support

4.2.6 Free Games Rating

For a particular reason, thousands of people access GP Store apps. Such people have their own history of this feature. Depending on this feedback, the consumer gives this program a star. In the GP shop, the ranking ratio was between 0 and 5. Level 0 in the ranking means that the code is really poor and score of 5 indicates that it is too perfect for usability. The ranking attribute was presented as a histogram, which showed how people view free games. Many game software consumers offer 4.5 stars to free applications visualized in the histogram as shown in Figure 35.

4.2.7 Paid Games Rating

It is shown in the histogram that the paid games are rated by the people differently. It is prominent in the visualization that most of the users rate paid games with rating score as 4.5. However, as compare to free games people do not hesitate to give 0 ratings in paid games to paid games because they buy that game and not satisfy by it.

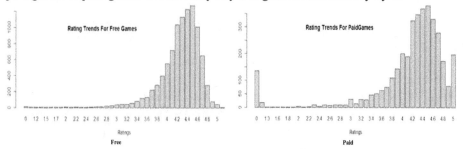

Figure 35 Rating Trends of Free and Paid Games

4.2.8 Analysis of Rating Attribute with Categories of Free Games

Games applications have different categories in GP store like Adventure, Arcade, Action, Board, Casino, Casual, Card, Educational, Music, Puzzle, Racing, Role_Playing, Sports, Strategy, Simulation, Trivia, Word. We visualize the rating through histogram as in visualization clearly define that card category has a high rating as shown in Figure 36.

4.2.9 Analysis of Rating Attribute with Categories of Paid Games

In this paper, we analyze the different applications for developers and users. So, in this analysis of rating is the more important thing because through rating we can judge the application demand in the market. Also, rating plays an important role in decision making for an application. We visualized the rating of the application through a histogram. The histogram analysis shows that the users give more rating to the puzzle games category.

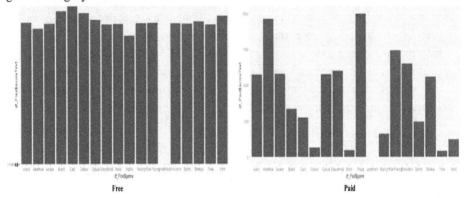

Free **Paid**

Figure 36 Analysis of Rating Attribute with Categories of Free and Paid Games

4.2.10 Analysis of Install Attribute with all Categories of Free Games

The demand for the application can be judged based on several installs. The number of installs of any application plays an important role to make the rough idea related to that application. It is demonstrated that how much installs of free games application concerning sub-categories of games application. In Figure 37 it is visualized that Arcade game category have maximum number of installs.

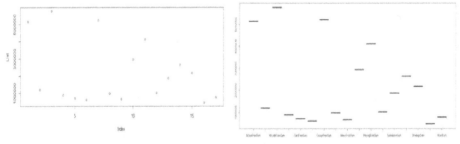

Figure 37 Analysis of Install Attribute with all Categories of Free Games

4.2.11 Analysis of Install Attribute with all Categories of Paid Games

The demand for the application can be judged based on several installs. The number of installs of any application plays an important role to make the rough idea related to that application. It is demonstrated that how much installs of paid games application concerning sub-categories of games application. In Figure 38 it is visualized that Arcade game category has a maximum number of installs.

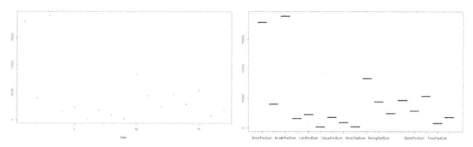

Figure 38 Analysis of Install Attribute with all Categories of Paid Games

4.2.12 Visualization of Different Attribute with Sub-Categories of Free and Paid Games

CIRCOS has been used to represent and evaluate free and paying program attributes, including four attributes Scores, IAP, Help Advertisements, and Installations. The CIRCOS is a method that can reliably classify many independent variables and dependent variables. The location of the item in the circular structure of the data may be easily defined. We have used the CIRCOS kit to display the details. CIRCOS shows the large data in the partnership and the principle for publishing content that defines symmetries between the values as shown in Figure 39. Throughout the CIRCOS simulation system, several implementations have such collections. The color percentile indicates the proportion of color abundance in figures for every measurement. The drawn components will adjust the direction, color and size, and increasing color class should be seen the color of any class can be used because there is no valid explanation for this configuration.

4.2.12.1 Percentile Configuration

This collection displays the color percentile used in statistics showing the amount below and provides a percentage of observations occurring in a category of observations.

4.2.12.2 Components Scaling Configuration

In this section, which components are drawn and change their scale, color, and orientation will adjust. It is important to get the ideogram layout right. For example, making all components appear to be the same size can emphasize the comparison between relative positions in patterns.

4.2.12.3 Colors Configuration

In colors block, we have all color definitions. In CIRCOS we have many color definitions like luminance-normalized colors, CSC chromosome color schemes,

Brewer palettes, pure colors and hues and so on. To add these configurations always having good reasons in our analysis and visualization. The pattern to import the colors_fonts_patterns.conf in the CIRCOS.conf. Importing this file will define patterns, fonts, colors and using an appropriate block structure.

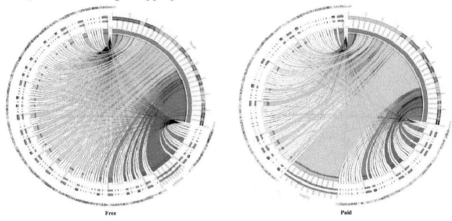

Free   Paid

Figure 39 Visualization of Four Attribute with sub-Categories of Free and Paid Games using CIRCOS

4.3   Discussion

Hundreds of developers and customers come to GP Store to access and upload software. Such implementations also involve gaming, school, films, etc. Both the programs submitted to the play shop also have two key forms which can be free and charged for. We have scrapped 550 applications for both free and paying group of games in this research report. In the final analysis of the data collection 10k free and 3600 paying application of various types of games are open. Adventures, Pinball, Game, Table, Casino, Casual, Card, Academic, Music, Games, Cycling, Role Playing, Sporting, Tactics, Training, Trivia and Word would be included in the specification. We also scrapped 70 separate attributes for each program, but in this study, we use four review attributes, namely Reviews, IAP, Advertisements and Installs. To evaluate the attributes and check the interaction between various attributes, RStudio and CIRCOS are used. In CIRCOS, the statistical details on the various libraries such as percentiles, elements, and colors test the specific settings.

4.4 Internet of Medical Things for Smart D3S to Enable Road Safety

4.4.1 Overview

Many collisions were found because of driver exhaustion. Drowsiness is a state of thinking until the driver falls unconscious such that the driver cannot carry out his acts accurately, such as automobile stopping and automobile motion tracking. In order to evaluate driver somnolence, we have developed an IoT enabled medical framework. A model was suggested and this situation was tested in the NS3 WSN modeling method. This analysis demonstrates that the incident level can be greatly reduced. If the drivers' somnolence is sensed, a warning alarm is issued by different sensor nodes to all those drivers that are near to the driver's sleep. The coordinated activity of sensor nodes is another special aspect of the sensor network. For Google Play estimation and review, a data collection in the division in medical applications was deleted. The scraping has been carried out with 550 applications for each medical device group. Nearly 70 attributes for each Google Play Store program have been omitted for each group.

4.5 Results and Discussion of Google Play Store Use Case

On Google Play Store, the creators of the Andriod program upload thousands of applications. Without supervision and balancing, consumers can access such applications without testing the program whether this program is appropriate for the consumer or not. False or malicious apps will take the user's personal details and destroy the user 's trust in the Google play stores. The validity of the application can not be calculated since the developers have no detail at the front end of the program. Even the Google Play Store has little details about the application's source code. We visualized InAppPurchases, the proportion of ads supports, reviews and downloads in Google Play Shop's portrayal of histogram free and paying medical group applications. We visualized the interaction between various CIRCOS attributes.

4.5.1 Free Medical Offering InApplicationPurchases

By purchasing a variety of medical apps in the Google Play Store for licenses, points, goods etc., these resources can be accessible to a customer when undertaking other tasks or events that may not necessarily affect the particular medical application. Of starters, certain medical apps offer coins only by buying a credit card, by filling in the survey form, by showing specific facts or photos, etc. Free apps also provide IAP, as no payment is paid by consumers of such programs when running free applications. We used Pie3D charts to represent the percentage of specified attributes. The ratio of such prescription services indicates the 15% free IAP and 85% free IAP did not bid as shown in Figure 40 (a).

4.5.2 Paid Medical Offering InApplicationPurchases

Paid programs bill money at deployment time, which is why such apps provide their customers with better convenience and satisfaction. The percentage of IAP sales in the paying program is smaller. We can show comparative statistics on paying IAP apps, Pie3D will view that only 5% of medical uses charged to provide IAP, while that 95% of compensated medical applications did not provide IAP as shown Figure 40 (b).

4.5.3 Free Medical Advertisements

Content plays a vital function in businesses' growth, labels and so on. Most apps include the advertisements of different businesses in Google Play Store, which often frustrate users and provides some useful details. In the deployment process, free apps did not charge any fees, and most apps offer ads. The pie3d graphs reveal only 23 per cent of free medical advertisements and just 77 per cent of free medical ads did not bid as shown in Figure 40 (c).

4.5.4 Paid Medical Advertisements

The pie3D chart shows that just 3% paid medical to offer advertisements, and 97% paid medical did not offer advertisements, as shown in Figure 40 (d). Thanks to the reality that paying programs incur those costs at deployment time. These advertisements frustrate the consumer of the program for a period, but the paying device owners maintain the client's comfort zone. The commercial level is smaller in paying apps relative to free applications.

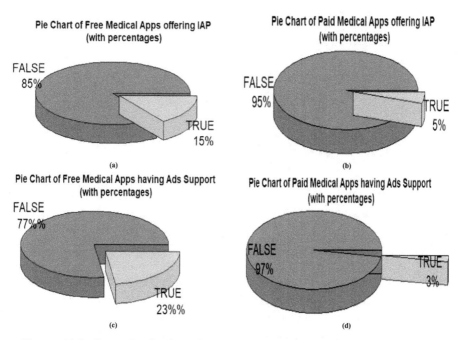

Figure 40 Different Medical Applications (a) Free IAP (b) Paid IAP (c) Free ads support (d) Paid ads support

4.5.5 Free Medical Rating Value

Hundreds of people purchase software for a common reason from Google Play Store. Such people have their own history of this feature. Depending on this feedback, the consumer gives this program a star. The scale of the ranking in Google Play Store is from 0 to 5. Score scale 0 means that this program is really poor, and a ranking scale of 5 indicates that the program is performance very fine. The ranking attribute has been visualized as a histogram which shows how people rate medication free of charge. Some medical uses offer an average of 4.2 for free software visualized in the histogram,as shown in Figure 41.

4.5.6 Paid Medical Rating Value

Histogram demonstrates how citizens perceive paying patient applications. It can be shown that most people often offer five stars for paying medical applications. By contrast to free medical application, though, consumers do not hesitate to offer zero scores for paying medical applications if they purchase and will not fulfill the demand.

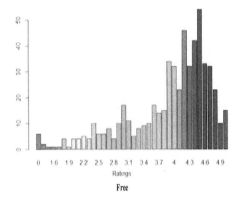

Ratings

Free   Paid

Figure 41 Free and Paid medical application rating trends

4.5.7 Free and Paid Medical Applications Installs

The number of apps deployed plays an significant part in demonstrating the success of the service. The image below displays certain free medical software in groups. As we can see, the free group has more downloads than certain groups, as shown in Figure 42. When we consider a category in Google Play Store that runs most of the time, we will direct developers in testing their talents in this area. The table below demonstrates several implementations with paying medical software related to divisions. As can be shown, the free group has a greater percentage than other tier installations, as shown in Figure 42.

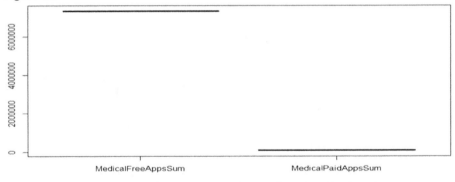

MedicalFreeAppsSum   MedicalPaidAppsSum

Figure 42 The number of installs for free and paid medical applications

4.5.8 CIRCOS Visualization for Free and Paid Medical Applications

We used CIRCOS to display and evaluate attributes of free and paying applications; we have four scores, IAP, ads and installs attributes. The CIRCOS market point of view is a method for quickly defining several contingent and independent variables. The location of the item in the circular structure of the data may be easily defined. We have used the CIRCOS kit to display the details. CIRCOS shows the broad data in the connecting ratio and the concept for publishing consistency that describes the symmetries between the values, as shown in Figure 43. The story is drawn from the amount of downloads and Google Play user scores for free and paying medical apps. Many apps provide in-app transactions and promotional assistance. The estimates for in-app sales and the availability of advertisements are very small as all characteristics in the apps are very low. Throughout the CIRCOS simulation system, several implementations have such collections. The color percentile indicates the proportion of color abundance in figures for every measurement. The constructed components that change the position, colour, and size, and any colour style will indicate that the material should be of any sort, and that this configuration should not be used for any purpose.

4.5.8.1 Configurations

While CIRCOS arranges this simulation, certain libraries often integrate such libraries to work differently. The value of such shades indicates the proportion of this value level in percentages in all displays. The color attracted components may adjust the direction, colour, colour, and even along with the settings would display any coloring that, along with any form, you would take advantage of such settings if you have no reasonable reason not to use.

4.5.8.2 Percentile Configuration

The book shows the viability of colour, which is only one move, which shows the value under a certain proportion of sayings in a collection of terms.

4.5.8.3 Components Scaling Configuration

In this section, we must correct the attractions of both sections and adjust their size, shade and orientation. It is important to locate the ideogram template correctly. By way of examples, the generation of all components tends to be exactly the same size will illustrate the difference between comparative design locations.

4.5.8.4 Colors Configuration

Only the <colors> section contains all the meanings for coloring. Circular data and knowledge analysis program (CIRCOS) has several common coloring concepts (pure colors, brake palettes, UCSC chromosome color schemes, light-type colours, etc.) When you don't have a perfect reason to ".conf" in your "CIRCOS.conf" you will still have them in your settings. This guide will be used to define fonts , colors and styles using the appropriate block layout.

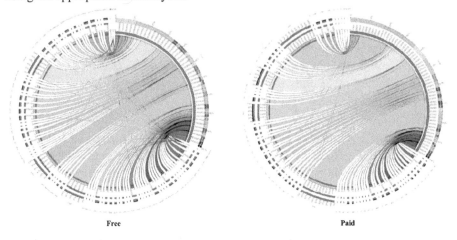

Figure 43 CIRCOS free and paid medical application visualization

4.6 Discussion

A driver's drowsiness identification program is built in the research report, which will help to avoid or reduce the number of accidents in Pakistan. D3S is reliable and cost-effective, a good quality webcam is required to monitor the driver's somnolence and processing network. The D3S research is performed with the MATLAB setting. The machine tests sleepiness based on the driver's eye closing state and provides about 85% precision. If the somnolence of any driver is detected, a warning alarm is given to all other drivers that are near to the sleeping person, and we use separate sensor nodes. The coordinated activity of sensor nodes is another special aspect of the sensor network. Sensor nodes have an on-board cpu. Education, military and defense are some of the fields of operation. For starters, a doctor may track the physiological data of a patient remotely. For calculation and comparison, we use the Google Play Scraper to create a Google Play Store Catalog of both free and paid medical apps. Through utilizing this scraper we are scraping at least 550 applications in free and paying applications for each type of medical use. We can scrape almost 70 attributes on each Google Play Store code, but we use four attributes for our study. We hope that, rather than the latest personal computers, wireless sensor networks should become an important part of our lives in the future.

4.7 Integration of Google Play Content and Frost Prediction using CNN: Events Data Collection using IoT Devices and their Detections

4.7.1 Overview

Frost forecasting involves dynamic decision making utilizing conditional probabilities. The production of crops and flowers is decreased because of frosts, so we must anticipate this in order to mitigate harm. When the effects of the frost forecast are correct, otherwise the frost loss can be may. A social learning method is used in this report in order to predict frost incidents using the Convolution Neural Network (CNN). We have used this to obtain more and more precise performance. Events of freezing need to be expected sooner in order to take precautionary steps on time. For Google Play calculation and review, we have therefore removed a data collection from various genres from agricultural fields, gathering top 550 applications for each type of agricultural applications with 70 attributes for each group. The forecast of frost occurrences with an accuracy of 98.86 per cent prior to the real frost occurrence.

4.8 Results and Discussion of Google Play Store Use Case

Google Play Store is the central repository for the web where millions of apps have been submitted by many developers. Millions of consumers often access such apps without testing the apps' reliability and duplicity. It creates customer failure because of consumer trust harm to the Google Play Shop. In addition, there is a limited amount of knowledge regarding these applications supported by Google Play Store. We have a Google Play Store server and a Google Play Scraper for free and paying agriculture apps. By using this scraper, the top 550 applications of each agricultural form are selected in a free and paying group of operation. That Google Play Store application has 70 rating tools, including InAppPurcahses, addSupported and the number of downloads. Example agriculture technology server screenshot. The findings of the study indicate the installations and scores of free and paid applications in the form of histograms, the purchasing price of such free and paid applications and the buying cost of the applications providing a proportion of the marketing subsidy for all types of agricultural use.

4.8.1 InApplicationPurchases (IAP) of free agricultural apps

Google Play Store sells points, items and so on in the program purchasing number of agricultural apps. The customer may access such resources by conducting other functions or events. Free apps primarily provide IAP as no payment is paid to the consumers of such programs when free apps are enabled. We used Pie3D charts to represent the percentage of the specified attributes. The proportion of agricultural implementations show that 19% of the IAP free agricultural bid and 81% of the IAP free agricultural bid did not offer IAP as shown in Figure 44 (a).

4.8.2 InApplicationPurchases (IAP) of paid agricultural apps

Paying agricultural applications normally charge money during installations; thus, such applications provide their consumers with more ease and satisfaction. The percentage of IAP sales is smaller in paying programs. We can see comparative statistics on paid IAP applications, Pie3D can see that 10% paying agricultural applications do not offer IAP and that only 90% paying agricultural applications do not give IAP as shown in Figure 44 (b).

4.8.3 Advertisements for free agricultural apps

Advertising plays a significant part in businesses and products' growth. Most apps in Google Play Store include advertisements from different entities that often frustrate the users and offer valuable details. During the point of launch, free software does not fee, which is why most apps provide ads. The pie3d diagrams reveal that 65% of free agricultural devices provide advertisements, while just 35% do not provide ads as shown in Figure 44 (c).

4.8.4 Advertisements for paid agricultural apps

The pie3D chart shows that just 12% paid agricultural apps to offer advertisements and 88% paid agricultural apps do not offer advertisements as shown in Figure 44 (d). Since at the point of deployment billing systems take those payments. These advertisements frustrate the consumer of the program for a period, but the paying device owners maintain the client's comfort zone. In premium applications, the commercial level is smaller than in free software.

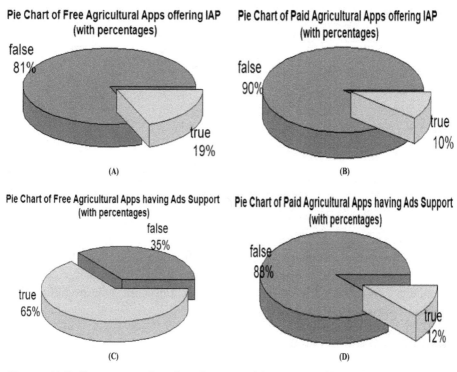

Pie Chart of Free Agricultural Apps offering IAP (with percentages)

false 81%

true 19%

(A)

Pie Chart of Paid Agricultural Apps offering IAP (with percentages)

false 90%

true 10%

(B)

Pie Chart of Free Agricultural Apps having Ads Support (with percentages)

false 35%

true 65%

(C)

Pie Chart of Paid Agricultural Apps having Ads Support (with percentages)

false 88%

true 12%

(D)

Figure 44 Different agricultural applications (a) Free IAP (b) Paid IAP (c) Free ads support (d) Paid ads support

4.8.5 Rating value of free agricultural apps

Hundreds of people purchase software for a common reason from Google Play Store. Such people have their own familiarity with every specific program. Depending on this feedback, the customer offers the program a ranking. The ranking ratio in Google Play Store was placed between 0 and 5. Zero ranking shows that this program is really poor and 5 indicates that the software is too good to use. The ranking attribute was presented as a histogram for free agricultural applications. Many users have provided 4.2 ratings for freely visualized applications in the histogram as shown in Figure 45.

4.8.6 Rating value of paid agricultural apps

This can be shown that most people offer 5 stars for paying applications. Nevertheless, the contrast with free apps makes it plain that users will not hesitate to offer 0 stars to premium applications as they purchase this product and are not pleased.

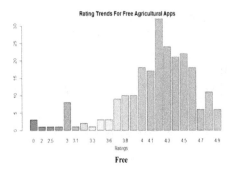

Figure 45 Free and Paid agricultural application Rating trends

4.8.7 Free and Paid agricultural Applications Installs

The number of installs in increasing program is a significant measure of the app's success. It is seen that several free agricultural applications are enabled. As we can see, the free group has more installations than other groups. Any implementations of paying agricultural devices have been reported. The group Unlimited software has a higher number of downloads as shown in Figure 46.

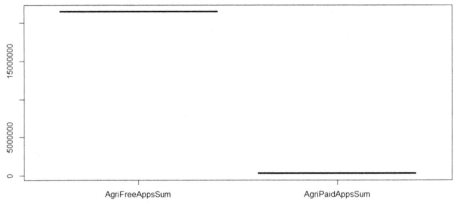

Figure 46 The number of installs for free and paid agricultural apps

4.9 Discussion

The output of crops and flowers is decreased due to frost events and this occurrence needs to be forecast in order to mitigate harm. In this article, we have provided a CNN model system for forecasting frost events and a conv1d framework for processing 1-dimensional results. We have essentially installed our sensors in the region, obtained the soil data and temperature, and forecast the cold events using the CNN model. We also used three convolution layers that are a more efficient process. Before that, we used bagging methodology to make our forecasts more precise using ensemble research. We also used three versions, a single layer is in one model, two layers in the second model and three layers in the third model. We integrated these factors into the ensemble model, took the forecast by the use of the packaging method and then checked the experiment. For estimation and study, we have also developed a Google Play Store list, which contains both free and paid agricultural applications utilizing the Google Play Scraper. By using this scraper, we have scraped the top 550 applications for free and paying applications in each agricultural domain segment. We have scrapped 70 attributes for each Google Play Store device, but in the future, we will use four attributes for our study and other attributes for certain kinds of checking.

4.10 The Experiences of user's positive and negative behavior toward various types of games application: A text mining approach

4.10.1 Overview

Google Play Store Apps tested by consumers play a significant role in creating electronic word of mouth, acting as an online networking platform that significantly affects users' appetite for game applications. We evaluate consumer feedback of game applications with latent semantical processing, a text mining technique.

4.11 Results and Discussion of Experiences of user's positive and negative behavior toward various types of games application

We consider that the determinants that generate good or harmful uses for game apps are diverse and are unique to categories of games, including small games, large/arena games and large-scale application/business applications and category of games. The analysis gives insight into the positivity and detrimental impact of gaming apps by enhancing the program and fulfilling users ' expectations for the various forms of software applications.

4.11.1 Factors leading to user positive and negative behavior toward each specific type of game application

This work provides both positive and negative reviews focused on the LSA, in order to recognize the variables that may influence the determinants of positive and negative judgments of consumers in all sorts of game applications. The key variables known in LSA and the favorable and derogatory elements of a user's ratings. The significance of each element is shown by the singular meaning in each row. This study states that 600 to 1500 words are used in each element and "fast loading terminology" as the top 10 words for presentation work picked. The findings of LSA demonstrate that these key variables encompass 95% of both relevant words and consumer ratings. This shows that all the characteristics of negative and optimistic feedback of each form of device can easily be expressed in these top variables as shown in Table 4 - Table 7.

4.11.2 Summary of determinants of user positiveness toward each type of game applications

The determinants of user positive in the context of different applications is generally identical to those of sports, game play initiative, game suggestion and game and graphics deals, many of which were addressed among the user positive considerations. While the crucial role of each customer has been diversified in the course of the different game applications. At the other side, each product form was subject to a supplementary user positive effect: successful application for large / arena games / big app / enterprise application; description of the user positive in each game category as shown in Table 8.

4.11.3 Summary of determinants of user negativeness toward each type of game applications

The negative determinants of consumers for the different forms of game applications is varied. These interconnected considerations include competition, competition commitment, game rating, and advertisement. In comparison, negative and positive variables were the most common and distinct determinants of negative characteristics across the various game applications as shown in Table 9.

Table 4 Determinants of User Positiveness towards mini games/small application

Determinants of User Positiveness			
Factors	Interpretations (Labels)	Singular Values	High-Loading Terms
Factors 1	Game enjoyment	3.515/3.306/3.633	Addictive, addictive_fun, awesome_positive, awesome, beauty, brilliant, brilliant_game, app_positive, cool_game
Factors 2	Effort for gameplay	2.718	complete_game, easy_positive, enjoy_app, enjoy_playing, game_amaz, game_awesom, game_challeng, game_complet, game_control
Factors 3	Game recommendation	5.43	enjoy_playing, addictive_fun, awesome, beauty, brilliant, brilliant_game, excelent_game, favorit, decent_definite
Factors 4	Offers in games	2.823	option_play, mode_posit, lot_ad, non_stop, given_star, online_play
Factors 5	Graphics	2.515	graphic_great, nice_graphic, game_graphic, nic_positive

Table 5 Determinants of User Dis-Positiveness towards mini games/small application

Determinants of User Dis-Positiveness			
Factors	**Interpretations (Labels)**	**Singular Values**	**High-Loading Terms**
Factors 1	Game Enjoyment	4.743/5.964	hate_game, app_plain, awkward, bad_posit, bore_game, disturb, game_hate, game_hate,
Factors 2	Game Play	2.515	odd_shape, gui_negativ, keep_mind, imposs, glitch, game_glitich, disappoint, fix_level, fix_problem, fix_level,
Factors 3	Game Recommendation	5.436	Disappoint, game_bad, game_hate, instal_neg,
Factors 4	Advertisement	5.03, 5.46*	level_ad, plai_ad, advertise_negative, game_advert, game_advertis *, lot_ad,

Table 6 Determinants of User Positiveness towards large/arena games/big application/enterprise app

Determinants of User Positiveness			
Factors	**Interpretations (Labels)**	**Singular Values**	**High-Loading Terms**
Factors 1	Game enjoyment	3.515/3.306/3.633	Addictive, addictive_fun, awsome_positive, awsome, beauti, brilliant, brilliant_game, app_positive, cool_game
Factors 2	Effort for gameplay	2.718	complete_game, easy_positive, enjoy_app, enjoy_playing, game_amaz, game_awesom, game_challeng, game_complet, game_control
Factors 3	Game recommendation	5.43	enjoy_playing, addictive_fun, awsome, beauti, brilliant, brilliant_game, excelent_game, favorit, decent_definite
Factors 4	Offers in games	2.823	option_plai, mode_posit, lot_ad, non_stop, given_star, onlin_plai
Factors 5	Graphics	2.515	graphic_great, nice_graphic, game_graphic, nic_positive

Table 7 Determinants of User Dis-Positiveness towards large/arena games/big application/enterprise app

Determinants of User Dis-Positiveness			
Factors	**Interpretations (Labels)**	**Singular Values**	**High-Loading Terms**
Factors 1	Game enjoyment	4.743/5.964	hate_game, app_plain, awkward, bad_posit, bore_game, disturb, game_hate, game_hate,
Factors 2	game play	2.515	odd_shape, gui_negativ, keep_mind, imposs, glitch, game_glitich, disappoint, fix_level, fix_problem, fix_level,
Factors 3	Game recommendation	5.436	Disappoint, game_bad, game_hate, instal_neg,
Factors 4	Advertisement	5.03, 5.46*	level_ad, plai_ad, advertise_negative, game_advert, game_advertis *, lot_ad,

Table 8 Determinant Factors of User Positiveness towards Each Type of Games

Factors	Reflections	Ranking			
		Full featured Game	Limited featured games	Games with inapppurchase and offers	Games without inapppurchase and offers
Game recommendation	Highly recommended, accessibility, easy to play	4	2	4	2
Game play	Story, category, interface,	4	2	3	1
Game rating	Race with fight(blur), level of game (low, moderate)	4	1	3	1
Offers in games	purchase items, gadgets,	3	1	3	1

Table 9 Determinant Factors of User Dis-Positiveness towards Each Type of Games

Factors	Reflections	Ranking			
		Full featured Game	Limited featured games	Games with inapppurchase and offers	Games without inapppurchase and offers
Advertisement	ads after end of game, ads to view and short bonuses	4	2	3	1
Inapppurchase	purchase things play next level, purchase specific things	4	1	4	2
Waiting for rejoin the game (Online game)	Wait to end the game	3	1	2	1

4.12 Discussion

LSA of online reviews of the user to the game application, this research is recognized and compared determinants of positive and negative behavior in the direction of large/arena games/big application/enterprise app, mini-games/small application. Toward of each Type of Games the main conclusion is the following: According to the first question of research, a research found that for each kind of game application, user positive and negative behavior determinants were diverse. Moderately, the determinants of user positiveness were more frequent and explained the center of applications. These determinants integrated as Game enjoyment, Effort for gameplay, Game recommendation, Offers in games and Graphics. Additionally, the determinants of user negativeness were more precise, including less Game Enjoyment, GamePlay, Game Recommendation, and Advertisement. Moreover, the research found that for every kind of game application, number of user's negativeness factors was higher than the number of user positiveness element, which explained that the cause of negativeness was more significant than the cause of positiveness for users staying in every kind of game application. According to the second question of research, the research found that for every kind of game application, determinants of user positive and negative behavior were not uniformly significant. Rankings of the significance can be rank for each factor that led to user positiveness, or negativeness were prearranged according to the singular values in Table 4 - Table 7.

According to the third question of research, the research found that type of determinants for user's positiveness was approximately similar for every kind of game application; these determinants had different raking of importance. The game recommendation was the most influential factor in determining user positiveness towards for large/arena games/big application/enterprise app, mini-games/small application, and towards Each Type of Games. Game enjoyment can play a most manipulating role in user positiveness toward large/arena games/big application/enterprise app and mini games/small application. Then, the research recognized an extra determinant of user positiveness toward each type of game application. Gameplay was imperative for users of large/arena games/big application/enterprise app, mini-games/small application, and towards Each Type of Games. A Graphics was necessary for large/arena games/big application/enterprise app, mini-games/small application users. For each determinant of user negativeness, the research found both kind and the rankings were dissimilar between diverse types of game applications. Amongst the diverse factors recognized as determinants of negativeness, Game Enjoyment, Gameplay, Game Recommendation, Advertisement, In-app-purchase and Waiting for rejoin the game (Online game) created the most significant amount of negativeness among users of large/arena games/big application/enterprise app, mini-games/small application and towards Each Type of Games.

4.13 Analytical Measurement and Visualization of Users' Reviews about Google Play Store Applications using Machine Learning Methods

4.13.1 Overview

The truth is very obvious that almost everyone around the world uses smartphone phones. Half of this planet's population is concerned with texts, social networking, sports, apps, etc. This online platform gives both free and paying entry. Users are allowed to import a variety of apps from predefined categories on the Google Play platform. We also effectively scrapped thousands of consumer comments and device scores in this study report. 148 user ratings from 14 groups have been downloaded. In fact, 506259 comments were obtained from the Google play store and we reviewed semantic of feedback of other apps to figure out if comments were positive or extremely critical. We analyzed the findings using numerous machine learning algorithms including Naïve Bayes, Random Forest and Logistic Regression. We have contrasted the Term Frequency (TF) and Inverse Document Frequency (IDF) measurements for various parameters, such as time, recall and F1. Such mathematical findings have been visualized in the context of a bar map. The study of each algorithm is carried out one by one in this paper and the findings are contrasted. Finally, we find that logistic regression is the right method for Google Play Store Review Analysis. Logistic regression provides the highest accuracy, retrieve and F1 values before and after data collection pre-processing.

4.14 Analytical Measurement and Visualization After Pre-Processing

There are comparative results from various algorithms focused on specific sections after pre-processing; the strongest algorithm used to evaluate and distinguish feedback is to be matched and discovered.

4.14.1 Naïve Bayes Multinomial

Naive Bayes is used to characterize high-dimensional training data sets. The existence of a certain element is believed to be independent of certain characteristics. Models and forecasts can be made easily. We've scraped 148 user ratings from 14 Google Play Store groups. There are 40 comments on one tab, and 506259 ratings received from Google Play Store. Apply the Naïve Bayes classification algorithm to the analysis dataset and have specific details on various TF and TF/IDF parameters. Find the consistency of the group specification description and locate precision, recall and F1 statistical knowledge by taking account of all such criteria to calculate the consistency of the dataset is shown in Table 10. However, the Naïve Bayes algorithm bar graph diagram demonstrates series1 the consistency of the Naïve Bayes algorithm, series2 demonstrates precision, series3 retrieves and series4 displays the calculation of the F1 value as shown in Figure 47.

Table 10 Statistical information of Naïve Bayes algorithm on TF and TF/IDF bases after Preprocessing

| Application Category | Naïve Bayes Multinomial | | | | | | | |
| | TF | | | | TF/IDF | | | |
	Accuracy	Precision	Recall	F1 score	Accuracy	Precision	Recall	F1 score
Sports	0.602	0.359	0.316	0.315	0.594	0.341	0.227	0.203

Communication	0.587	0.333	0.332	0.304	0.597	0.297	0.301	0.254
Action	0.691	0.334	0.294	0.288	0.686	0.297	0.231	0.215
Arcade	0.725	0.283	0.231	0.235	0.737	0.319	0.191	0.168
Video players & editors	0.676	0.331	0.306	0.294	0.67	0.314	0.233	0.215
Weather	0.662	0.329	0.261	0.266	0.642	0.301	0.194	0.168
Card	0.689	0.31	0.285	0.276	0.68	0.28	0.227	0.209
Photography	0.696	0.367	0.327	0.31	0.705	0.362	0.276	0.248
Shopping	0.667	0.358	0.341	0.321	0.678	0.299	0.316	0.289
Health & fitness	0.788	0.273	0.212	0.218	0.811	0.208	0.194	0.177
Finance	0.532	0.301	0.287	0.266	0.557	0.284	0.258	0.226
Casual	0.73	0.334	0.285	0.288	0.745	0.334	0.205	0.182
Medical	0.745	0.359	0.272	0.279	0.753	0.338	0.204	0.181
Racing	0.718	0.357	0.278	0.285	0.72	0.331	0.218	0.201

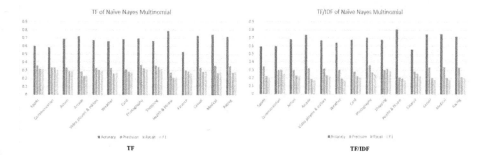

Figure 47 Bar chart visualization of TF (Term Frequency) and TF/IDF (Term Frequency/ Inverse Document Frequency) of Naïve Bayes algorithm after Preprocessing

4.14.2 Random Forest Algorithm

The Random Forests Classifier is the class of all methods specifically developed for decision tree applications. It generates a wide number of decision tree based on a random data collection and a random choice of variables. We've scraped 148 user ratings from 14 Google Play Store groups. There are 40 comments on one tab, and 506259 ratings received from Google Play Store. Apply the classification Random Forest algorithm on the analysis dataset to see specific details on various TF to TF / IDF parameters. Find the consistency of the group specification description and locate precision, recall and F1 statistical knowledge by taking account of all such criteria to calculate the consistency of the dataset as shown in Table 11. The Random Forest algorithm in which series 1 shows Random Forest algorithm accuracy, series2 shows precision, series3 shows recall and series4 shows the calculated value of F1 as shown in Figure 48.

85

Table 11 Statistical information of the Random Forest algorithm on TF and TF/IDF bases after Preprocessing

Application Category	Random Forest							
	TF				TF/IDF			
	Accuracy	Precision	Recall	F1 score	Accuracy	Precision	Recall	F1 score
Sports	0.585	0.34	0.312	0.308	0.589	0.344	0.308	0.304
Communication	0.544	0.314	0.313	0.294	0.545	0.307	0.312	0.288
Action	0.683	0.338	0.31	0.308	0.691	0.347	0.306	0.302
Arcade	0.721	0.32	0.27	0.274	0.729	0.334	0.262	0.269
Video players &editors	0.664	0.347	0.313	0.304	0.664	0.34	0.304	0.295
Weather	0.632	0.285	0.243	0.248	0.638	0.305	0.252	0.255
Card	0.665	0.312	0.285	0.279	0.673	0.321	0.284	0.277
Photography	0.683	0.353	0.32	0.312	0.69	0.352	0.315	0.301
Shopping	0.648	0.354	0.333	0.324	0.653	0.359	0.33	0.316
Health & fitness	0.765	0.324	0.248	0.254	0.779	0.315	0.235	0.24
Finance	0.517	0.309	0.291	0.27	0.52	0.31	0.293	0.27
Casual	0.728	0.341	0.284	0.292	0.732	0.342	0.274	0.28
Medical	0.729	0.33	0.28	0.285	0.739	0.336	0.265	0.271
Racing	0.714	0.359	0.317	0.319	0.724	0.37	0.306	0.311

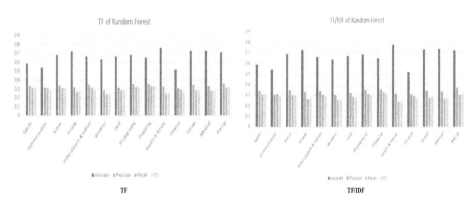

Figure 48 Bar chart visualization of TF (Term Frequency) and TF/IDF (Term Frequency/ Inverse Document Frequency) of the Random Forest algorithm after preprocessing

4.14.3 Logistic Regression Algorithm

In mathematics, the logistic model is a trustworthy mathematical form that simulates a binary deciding factor of its simple nature, utilizing the logistic functionality; other specific extensions occur. Back in the regression analysis, logistic regression calculates the logistic variant parameters; all binomial regressions are added. We've scraped 148 user ratings from 14 Google Play Store groups. There are 40 comments on one tab, and

506259 ratings received from Google Play Store. Apply the classification Random Forest algorithm on the analysis dataset to see specific details on various TF to TF / IDF parameters. Find the consistency of the group specification description and locate precision , recall and F1 statistical knowledge by taking account of all such criteria to calculate the consistency of the dataset as shown in Table 12. In comparison, the bar charts display the practical regression method under which the accuracy of the logistic regression method is shown in series 1, series2 shows the accuracy, series3 alert and series4 shows the F1 calculation as shown in Figure 49.

Table 12 Statistical information of Logistic Regression algorithm on TF and TF/IDF bases after Preprocessing

Application Category	Logistic Regression							
	TF				TF/IDF			
	Accuracy	Precision	Recall	F1 score	Accuracy	Precision	Recall	F1 score
Sports	0.622	0.414	0.343	0.343	0.621	0.404	0.319	0.315
Communication	0.585	0.349	0.329	0.32	0.599	0.352	0.327	0.301
Action	0.707	0.395	0.312	0.313	0.71	0.38	0.299	0.293
Arcade	0.744	0.353	0.262	0.266	0.747	0.351	0.25	0.252
Video players & editors	0.684	0.37	0.306	0.304	0.687	0.352	0.289	0.276
Weather	0.667	0.379	0.288	0.299	0.667	0.421	0.262	0.265
Card	0.696	0.379	0.301	0.305	0.698	0.344	0.283	0.271`
Photography	0.703	0.391	0.321	0.315	0.71	0.405	0.311	0.297
Shopping	0.67	0.407	0.342	0.336	0.682	0.444	0.332	0.315
Health & fitness	0.796	0.38	0.278	0.295	0.801	0.391	0.23	0.235
Finance	0.592	0.352	0.311	0.303	0.593	0.353	0.298	0.276
Casual	0.747	0.381	0.29	0.302	0.753	0.364	0.277	0.28
Medical	0.754	0.401	0.277	0.288	0.759	0.459	0.244	0.245
Racing	0.737	0.428	0.312	0.318	0.74	0.401	0.295	0.297

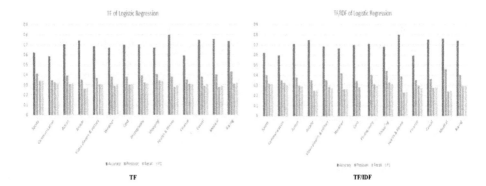

Figure 49 Bar chart visualization of TF (Term Frequency) and TF/IDF (Term Frequency/ Inverse Document Frequency) of Logistic Regression algorithm after preprocessing

4.14.4 Concluded Results of after preprocessing

This online platform has given consumers with free and paying entry. Users will select from over a million applications in different predefined categories in the Google Play Store. Hundreds of thousands of users' comments and device scores were discarded in this study. 148 user reviews from 14 groups were downloaded and 506259 feedback from the Google play store were obtained. Evaluated the findings using different algorithms for the analysis of computers, such as Naïve Bayes, Random Forest and Logistic Regression algorithms that enable users to verify if their measurements are strong, poor, average, etc. Calculated Term Frequency (TF) and Inverse Document Frequency (IDF) with various parameters, such as accuracy, recall and f1 value, contrasted the statistical effects of these algorithms with the preprocessing of the Raw analysis. Such statistical findings were visualized in the context of a bar map as shown in Figure 50 and Figure 51. In contrast, the logistic regression algorithm was tested as the best algorithm to track the semanticization of every analysis by Google application users on both TF and TF / IDF bases. As in the TF base sport division, it was seen that the logistic regression method is 0.622% accurate, 0.414% accurate, 0.343% recall and 0.343% F1 performance and statistical details for another test level as shown in Table 13. Furthermore, in TF / IDF the pragmatic regression method has 0.621% accuracy, 0.404% accuracy, 0.319% recall and 0.3150% F1 and statistical knowledge for another domain type as shown in Table 14.

Table 13 Statistical information compared with the different algorithm on TF bases after Preprocessing

Application Category	Naïve Bayes Accuracy	Random Forest Accuracy	Logistic Regression Accuracy	Naïve Bayes Precision	Random Forest Precision	Logistic Regression Precision	Naïve Bayes Recall	Random Forest Recall	Logistic Regression Recall	Naïve Bayes F1 score	Random Forest F1 score	Logistic Regression F1 score
Sports	0.602	0.585	0.622	0.359	0.34	0.414	0.316	0.312	0.343	0.315	0.308	0.343
Communication	0.587	0.544	0.585	0.333	0.314	0.349	0.332	0.313	0.329	0.304	0.294	0.32
Action	0.691	0.683	0.707	0.334	0.338	0.395	0.294	0.31	0.312	0.288	0.308	0.313
Arcade	0.725	0.721	0.744	0.283	0.32	0.353	0.231	0.27	0.262	0.235	0.274	0.266
Video players & editors	0.676	0.664	0.684	0.331	0.347	0.37	0.306	0.313	0.306	0.294	0.304	0.304
Weather	0.662	0.632	0.667	0.329	0.285	0.379	0.261	0.243	0.288	0.266	0.248	0.299
Card	0.689	0.665	0.696	0.31	0.312	0.379	0.285	0.285	0.301	0.276	0.279	0.305
Photography	0.696	0.683	0.703	0.367	0.353	0.391	0.327	0.32	0.321	0.31	0.312	0.315
Shopping	0.667	0.648	0.67	0.358	0.354	0.407	0.341	0.333	0.342	0.321	0.324	0.336
Health & fitness	0.788	0.765	0.796	0.273	0.324	0.38	0.212	0.248	0.278	0.218	0.254	0.295
Finance	0.532	0.517	0.592	0.301	0.309	0.352	0.287	0.291	0.311	0.266	0.27	0.303
Casual	0.73	0.728	0.747	0.334	0.341	0.381	0.285	0.284	0.29	0.288	0.292	0.302
Medical	0.745	0.729	0.754	0.359	0.33	0.401	0.272	0.28	0.277	0.279	0.285	0.288
Racing	0.718	0.714	0.737	0.357	0.359	0.428	0.278	0.317	0.312	0.285	0.319	0.318

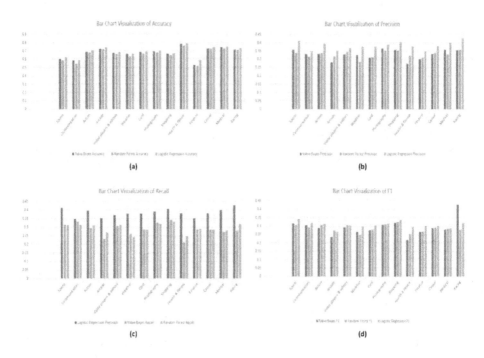

Figure 50 Bar chart visualization of Statistical information compared with the different algorithm on TF bases after Preprocessing

Table 14 Statistical information compared with the different algorithm on TF/IDF bases after Preprocessing

Application Category	Naïve Bayes Accuracy	Random Forest Accuracy	Logistic Regression Accuracy	Naïve Bayes Precision	Random Forest Precision	Logistic Regression Precision	Naïve Bayes Recall	Random Forest Recall	Logistic Regression Recall	Naïve Bayes F1 score	Random Forest F1 score	Logistic Regression F1 score
Sports	0.594	0.589	0.621	0.341	0.344	0.404	0.227	0.308	0.319	0.203	0.304	0.315
Communication	0.597	0.545	0.599	0.297	0.307	0.352	0.301	0.312	0.327	0.254	0.288	0.301
Action	0.686	0.691	0.71	0.297	0.347	0.38	0.231	0.306	0.299	0.215	0.302	0.293
Arcade	0.737	0.729	0.747	0.319	0.334	0.351	0.191	0.262	0.25	0.168	0.269	0.252

Video players & editors	0.67	0.664	0.687	0.314	0.34	0.352	0.233	0.304	0.289	0.215	0.295	0.276
Weather	0.642	0.638	0.667	0.301	0.305	0.421	0.194	0.252	0.262	0.168	0.255	0.265
Card	0.68	0.673	0.698	0.28	0.321	0.344	0.227	0.284	0.283	0.209	0.277	0.271`
Photography	0.705	0.69	0.71	0.362	0.352	0.405	0.276	0.315	0.311	0.248	0.301	0.297
Shopping	0.678	0.653	0.682	0.299	0.359	0.444	0.316	0.33	0.332	0.289	0.316	0.315
Health & fitness	0.811	0.779	0.801	0.208	0.315	0.391	0.194	0.235	0.23	0.177	0.24	0.235
Finance	0.557	0.52	0.593	0.284	0.31	0.353	0.258	0.293	0.298	0.226	0.27	0.276
Casual	0.745	0.732	0.753	0.334	0.342	0.364	0.205	0.274	0.277	0.182	0.28	0.28
Medical	0.753	0.739	0.759	0.338	0.336	0.459	0.204	0.265	0.244	0.181	0.271	0.245
Racing	0.72	0.724	0.74	0.331	0.37	0.401	0.218	0.306	0.295	0.201	0.311	0.297

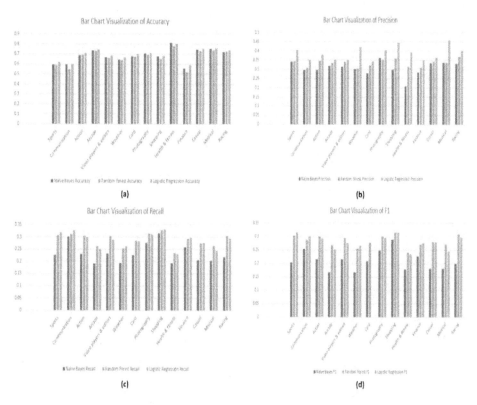

Figure 51 Bar chart visualization of Statistical information compared with the different algorithm on TF/IDF bases after Preprocessing

4.15 Analytical Measurement and Visualization After Data Collection

These are the statistical information of different algorithm on the base of the different paraments after data collection; compare and find the best algorithm that uses for the analysis and classification of reviews.

4.15.1 Naïve Bayes Multinomial

We've scraped 148 user ratings from 14 Google Play Store groups. There are 40 comments on one tab, and 506259 ratings received from Google Play Store. Apply the Naïve Bayes classification algorithm to the analysis dataset and have specific details on various TF and TF/IDF parameters. Find the consistency of the group specification description and locate precision , recall and F1 statistical knowledge by taking account of all such criteria to calculate the consistency of the dataset as shown in Table 15. However, the Naïve Bayes algorithm bar graph diagram demonstrates series1 the consistency of the Naïve Bayes algorithm, series2 demonstrates precision, series3 retrieves and series4 displays the calculation of the F1 value. as shown in Figure 52.

Table 15 Statistical information of Naïve Bayes algorithm on TF and TF/IDF bases after data collection

Application Category	Naïve Bayes Multinomial							
	TF				TF/IDF			
	Accuracy	Precision	Recall	F1 score	Accuracy	Precision	Recall	F1 score
Sports	0.607	0.368	0.335	0.334	0.593	0.328	0.221	0.194
Communication	0.584	0.334	0.337	0.311	0.597	0.292	0.302	0.255
Action	0.689	0.336	0.303	0.297	0.683	0.329	0.227	0.208
Arcade	0.724	0.273	0.221	0.227	0.737	0.33	0.191	0.168
Video players & editors	0.681	0.346	0.325	0.312	0.669	0.281	0.229	0.208
Weather	0.669	0.327	0.276	0.281	0.641	0.306	0.19	0.161
Card	0.689	0.282	0.305	0.272	0.68	0.29	0.223	0.205
Photography	0.691	0.366	0.335	0.317	0.707	0.367	0.279	0.25
Shopping	0.663	0.364	0.352	0.333	0.679	0.365	0.319	0.292
Health & fitness	0.788	0.277	0.218	0.225	0.811	0.2	0.194	0.176
Finance	0.536	0.312	0.297	0.277	0.554	0.261	0.257	0.226
Casual	0.727	0.338	0.304	0.306	0.745	0.31	0.204	0.181
Medical	0.749	0.348	0.29	0.298	0.753	0.38	0.203	0.18
Racing	0.717	0.351	0.289	0.297	0.718	0.359	0.214	0.195

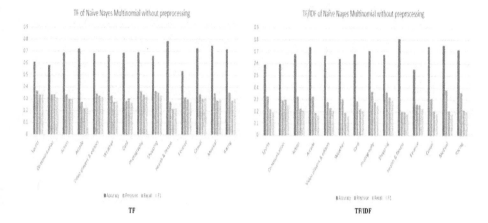

Figure 52 Bar chart visualization of TF (Term Frequency) and TF/IDF (Term Frequency/ Inverse Document Frequency) of Naïve Bayes algorithm after data collection

4.15.2 Random Forest Algorithm

We've scraped 148 user ratings from 14 Google Play Store groups. There are 40 comments on one tab, and 506259 ratings received from Google Play Store. Apply the classification Random Forest algorithm on the analysis dataset to see specific details on various TF to TF / IDF parameters. Find the consistency of the group specification description and locate precision , recall and F1 statistical knowledge by taking account of all such criteria to calculate the consistency of the dataset as shown in Table 16. The Random Forest algorithm in which series 1 shows Random Forest algorithm accuracy, series2 shows precision, series3 shows recall and series4 shows the calculated value of F1 as shown in Figure 53.

Table 16 Statistical information of the Random Forest algorithm on TF and TF/IDF bases after data collection

Application Category	Random Forest							
	TF				TF/IDF			
	Accuracy	Precision	Recall	F1 score	Accuracy	Precision	Recall	F1 score
Sports	0.589	0.359	0.311	0.314	0.595	0.352	0.307	0.309
Communication	0.559	0.321	0.314	0.296	0.555	0.32	0.309	0.29
Action	0.686	0.35	0.307	0.308	0.695	0.369	0.306	0.307
Arcade	0.725	0.338	0.265	0.275	0.729	0.336	0.256	0.265
Video players & editors	0.665	0.351	0.311	0.308	0.665	0.335	0.306	0.298

Weather	0.641	0.335	0.273	0.282	0.647	0.323	0.255	0.264
Card	0.666	0.325	0.28	0.281	0.669	0.322	0.274	0.273
Photography	0.689	0.372	0.328	0.321	0.69	0.363	0.318	0.308
Shopping	0.654	0.37	0.333	0.325	0.653	0.361	0.328	0.315
Health & fitness	0.778	0.299	0.215	0.22	0.788	0.354	0.22	0.225
Finance	0.532	0.311	0.292	0.276	0.529	0.317	0.294	0.272
Casual	0.735	0.345	0.273	0.284	0.739	0.346	0.267	0.277
Medical	0.737	0.342	0.276	0.284	0.743	0.351	0.259	0.268
Racing	0.719	0.361	0.311	0.317	0.726	0.383	0.307	0.317

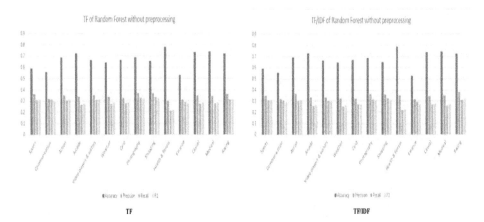

Figure 53 Bar chart visualization of TF (Term Frequency) and TF/IDF (Term Frequency/ Inverse Document Frequency) of the Random Forest algorithm after data collection

4.15.3 Logistic Regression Algorithm

We've scraped 148 user ratings from 14 Google Play Store groups. There are 40 comments on one tab, and 506259 ratings received from Google Play Store. Apply the classification Random Forest algorithm on the analysis dataset to see specific details on various TF to TF / IDF parameters. Find the consistency of the group specification description and locate precision , recall and F1 statistical knowledge by taking account of all such criteria to calculate the consistency of the dataset as shown in Table 17. In comparison, the bar charts display the practical regression method under which the accuracy of the logistic regression method is shown in series 1, series2 shows the accuracy, series3 alert and series4 shows the F1 calculation as shown in Figure 54.

Table 17 Statistical information of Logistic Regression algorithm on TF and TF/IDF bases after data collection

Application Category	Logistic Regression							
	TF				TF/IDF			
	accuracy	Precision	recall	F1 score	accuracy	Precision	recall	F1 score
Sports	0.623	0.416	0.35	0.353	0.629	0.416	0.331	0.328
Communication	0.588	0.355	0.334	0.326	0.602	0.361	0.334	0.312
Action	0.71	0.405	0.32	0.324	0.712	0.398	0.304	0.299
Arcade	0.744	0.369	0.271	0.278	0.747	0.349	0.246	0.247
Video Players & Editors	0.69	0.39	0.323	0.323	0.693	0.375	0.3	0.291
Weather	0.674	0.386	0.303	0.316	0.674	0.384	0.275	0.282
Card	0.697	0.373	0.306	0.31	0.699	0.359	0.288	0.281
Photography	0.707	0.403	0.332	0.328	0.714	0.422	0.322	0.309
Shopping	0.674	0.411	0.351	0.346	0.686	0.444	0.339	0.324
Health & Fitness	0.794	0.369	0.28	0.295	0.803	0.363	0.232	0.239
Finance	0.595	0.363	0.319	0.314	0.604	0.401	0.308	0.29
Casual	0.747	0.385	0.3	0.314	0.755	0.385	0.28	0.285
Medical	0.757	0.41	0.295	0.31	0.759	0.468	0.246	0.249
Racing	0.738	0.419	0.317	0.325	0.74	0.391	0.295	0.297

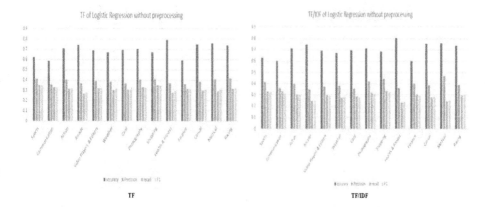

Figure 54 Bar chart visualization of TF (Term Frequency) and TF/IDF (Term Frequency/ Inverse Document Frequency) of Logistic Regression algorithm after data collection

4.15.4 Concluded Results of after data collection

We have 148 user feedback from 14 groups downloaded and have 506259 ratings received from the Google Play Store. Assess outcomes with the use of various machine learning algorithms such as Naïve Bayes, Random Forest and Logistic Regression algorithms, which will verify whether consumers have positive, poor, regular feedback and so on in the nature of comments for such applications. Calculating the Term

Frequency (TF) and Inverse Document Frequency (IDF) after the data collection of raw feedback contrasted the statistical effects of such algorithms, utilizing different criteria such as consistency, precision, recall , and F1 performance. Such statistical findings were visualized in the context of a bar map, as shown in Figure 55 and Figure 56. Following reference, evaluate the right algorithm for logistic regression to test the semantic analysis of every user's evaluation of Google apps on both TF and TF/IDF bases. As for the sports division in the TF foundation, logistic regression algorithms have an accuracy of 0.623%, an accuracy of 0.416%, a 0.35% recall, an F1 value of 0.35%, among other types of statistics, as shown in Table 18. In comparison, TF / IDF bases indicate that the algorithm of logistic regression is 0.629% accurate, 0.416% accurate, 0.331% remembered, and a 0.328% F1 value and the statistical results for another function type as shown in Table 19.

Table 18 Statistical information compared with the different algorithm on TF bases after data collection

Application Category	Naïve Bayes Accuracy	Random Forest Accuracy	Logistic Regression Accuracy	Naïve Bayes Precision	Random Forest Precision	Logistic Regression Precision	Naïve Bayes Recall	Random Forest Recall	Logistic Regression Recall	Naïve Bayes F1 score	Random Forest F1 score	Logistic Regression F1 score
Sports	0.607	0.589	0.623	0.368	0.359	0.416	0.314	0.314	0.35	0.334	0.314	0.353
Communication	0.584	0.559	0.588	0.334	0.321	0.355	0.296	0.296	0.334	0.311	0.296	0.326
Action	0.689	0.686	0.71	0.336	0.35	0.405	0.308	0.308	0.32	0.297	0.308	0.324
Arcade	0.724	0.725	0.744	0.273	0.338	0.369	0.275	0.275	0.271	0.227	0.275	0.278
Video players & editors	0.681	0.665	0.69	0.346	0.351	0.39	0.308	0.308	0.323	0.312	0.308	0.323
Weather	0.669	0.641	0.674	0.327	0.335	0.386	0.282	0.282	0.303	0.281	0.282	0.316
Card	0.689	0.666	0.697	0.282	0.325	0.373	0.281	0.281	0.306	0.272	0.281	0.31
Photography	0.691	0.689	0.707	0.366	0.372	0.403	0.321	0.321	0.332	0.317	0.321	0.328
Shopping	0.663	0.654	0.674	0.364	0.37	0.411	0.325	0.325	0.351	0.333	0.325	0.346
Health & fitness	0.788	0.778	0.794	0.277	0.299	0.369	0.22	0.22	0.28	0.225	0.22	0.295
Finance	0.536	0.532	0.595	0.312	0.311	0.363	0.276	0.276	0.319	0.277	0.276	0.314
Casual	0.727	0.735	0.747	0.338	0.345	0.385	0.284	0.284	0.3	0.306	0.284	0.314
Medical	0.749	0.737	0.757	0.348	0.342	0.41	0.284	0.284	0.295	0.298	0.284	0.31
Racing	0.717	0.719	0.738	0.351	0.361	0.419	0.317	0.317	0.317	0.297	0.317	0.325

Table 19 Statistical information compared with the different algorithm on TF/IDF bases after data collection

Application Category	Naïve Bayes Accuracy	Random Forest Accuracy	Logistic Regression Accuracy	Naïve Bayes Precision	Random Forest Precision	Logistic Regression Precision	Naïve Bayes Recall	Random Forest Recall	Logistic Regression Recall	Naïve Bayes F1 score	Random Forest F1 score	Logistic Regression F1 score
Sports	0.593	0.595	0.629	0.328	0.352	0.416	0.221	0.307	0.331	0.194	0.309	0.328
Communication	0.597	0.555	0.602	0.292	0.32	0.361	0.302	0.309	0.334	0.255	0.29	0.312
Action	0.683	0.695	0.712	0.329	0.369	0.398	0.227	0.306	0.304	0.208	0.307	0.299
Arcade	0.737	0.729	0.747	0.33	0.336	0.349	0.191	0.256	0.246	0.168	0.265	0.247
Video players & editors	0.669	0.665	0.693	0.281	0.335	0.375	0.229	0.306	0.3	0.208	0.298	0.291
Weather	0.641	0.647	0.674	0.306	0.323	0.384	0.19	0.255	0.275	0.161	0.264	0.282
Card	0.68	0.669	0.699	0.29	0.322	0.359	0.223	0.274	0.288	0.205	0.273	0.281
Photography	0.707	0.69	0.714	0.367	0.363	0.422	0.279	0.318	0.322	0.25	0.308	0.309
Shopping	0.679	0.653	0.686	0.365	0.361	0.444	0.319	0.328	0.339	0.292	0.315	0.324
Health & fitness	0.811	0.788	0.803	0.2	0.354	0.363	0.194	0.22	0.232	0.176	0.225	0.239
Finance	0.554	0.529	0.604	0.261	0.317	0.401	0.257	0.294	0.308	0.226	0.272	0.29
Casual	0.745	0.739	0.755	0.31	0.346	0.385	0.204	0.267	0.28	0.181	0.277	0.285
Medical	0.753	0.743	0.759	0.38	0.351	0.468	0.203	0.259	0.246	0.18	0.268	0.249
Racing	0.718	0.726	0.74	0.359	0.383	0.391	0.214	0.307	0.295	0.195	0.317	0.297

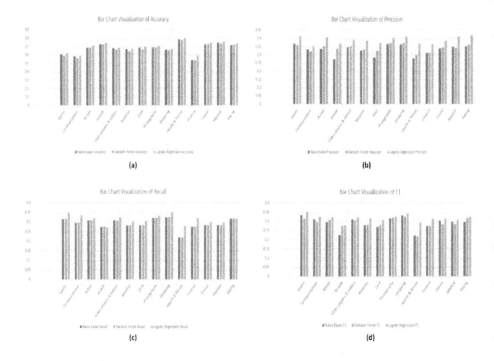

Figure 55 Bar chart visualization of Statistical information compared with the different algorithm on TF bases after data collection

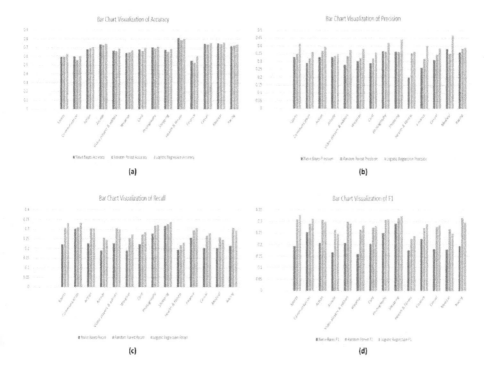

Figure 56 Bar chart visualization of Statistical information compared with the different algorithm on TF/IDF bases after data collection

4.16 Semantic analysis of Google play store applications reviews using Logistic Regression Algorithm

Following the examination of the different paragraphs, analyze that the logistic regression algorithm is the highest precision algorithm. In this section, analyze and classify all reviews in positive, negative and neutral classes. Set the target value if the comment value is positive, if the review is negative, it is equal to 1 and equal to 0. Also, analyze the neutral class with the trusted rate if the trust rate is between 0 and 1, then classify it as neutral. Different parameters such as application category, application name, application ID, reviews and ratings in our dataset, as shown in Figure 57. However, for checking the semantics of each review, these parameters are more enough. That is why drop some paraments and select only reviews of all application.

99

	Cetagory	App_Name	App_ID	Reviews	Rating
1					
2	Sports	Billiards City	com.billiards.city.pool.nation.club	Wonderfull App. Completed all 1020 levels, Can'	5
3	Sports	Billiards City	com.billiards.city.pool.nation.club	It's good, I like the gameplay. Please change up t	4
4	Sports	Billiards City	com.billiards.city.pool.nation.club	I really enjoyed this game until I saw one of the ¡	1
5	Sports	Billiards City	com.billiards.city.pool.nation.club	PLEASE!!! Get rid of the odd shaped tables and g	1
6	Communication	Hangouts Dialer	com.google.android.apps.hangoutsdialer	st from the notification menu\u003c/\u003e Oth:	3
7	Communication	Hangouts Dialer	com.google.android.apps.hangoutsdialer	Wish I found it earlier!!!	5
8	Communication	Hangouts Dialer	com.google.android.apps.hangoutsdialer	sage\u003c/\u003e I love it I dont even have to p	5
9	Communication	Hangouts Dialer	com.google.android.apps.hangoutsdialer	Wanted to make video calling as moto g phone c	1
10	Arcade	Leps World 2	at.ner.lepsWorld2	It is a good time disaster	5
11	Arcade	Leps World 2	at.ner.lepsWorld2	It is so nise I have never seen before	5
12	Arcade	Leps World 2	at.ner.lepsWorld2	I played it totally more than 3 times	5
13	Arcade	Leps World 2	at.ner.lepsWorld2	Is awesome cool game love it some time you lov	5
14	Video Players & Editors	Youtube	com.google.android.youtube	Excellent App	5
15	Video Players & Editors	Youtube	com.google.android.youtube	Very nice	5
16	Video Players & Editors	Youtube	com.google.android.youtube	Very good	4
17	action	WARSHIP BATTLE	com.joycity.warshipbattle	The best at all features this game... Very nice....	5
18	action	WARSHIP BATTLE	com.joycity.warshipbattle	I love this game good work	5
19	action	WARSHIP BATTLE	com.joycity.warshipbattle	I like it	4
20	Weather	NOAA Weather Radar & Alerts	com.apalon.weatherradar.free	Just better than the rest, period.	5
21	Weather	NOAA Weather Radar & Alerts	com.apalon.weatherradar.free	Great tool for the road or around town.	5
22	photography	Sweet Selfie	com.cam001.selfie	It's a very good app	5

Figure 57 Sample screenshot of the original dataset that scrapped

4.16.1 Data preparation and cleaning of reviews

4.16.1.1 HTML decoding

To convert HTML encoding into text and to '&amp,' '\amp' & 'quot' at start and ending in the text field.

4.16.1.2 Data Preparation 2: '#' mention

"#" carries import information which needs to be dealt with.

4.16.1.3 URL links

Delete all URLs in the posts that tend to disable them.

4.16.1.4 UTF-8 BOM (Byte Order Mark)

For character designs such as "\xef\xbf\xbd," these are UTF-8 BOMs. It's a byte sequence (EF BB BF) that enables readers to identify the UTF-8 file.

4.16.1.5 Hashtag / Numbers

Text of Hashtag may provide valuable comment information. It may be a little hard to get rid of the entire text with the "#" or a number or any other unique character.

~ is the element not appropriate for excluding them in the study?

4.16.1.7 Tokenizing and joining

Parse the entire comment into small pieces and fuse again. After applying the above cleaning rules, the reviews have been cleaned up, as shown in Figure 58.

	Reviews
1	
2	wonderfull app completed all levels can not wait for more levels level has bug but you can get around it to complete
3	it good like the gameplay please change up the music as it gets repetitive after the nd level and you can hear the t
4	really enjoyed this game until saw one of the adverts throughout the ngame with man and woman spooning it is ha
5	please get rid of the odd shaped tables and go back to the classic table please fix level where the balls and cue st
6	very easy game to play and has actually given me pointers on how to play nreal game of pool like where to hit the
7	not going to lie just started playing this game probably about hours ago and am thoroughly addicted it pretty awesi
8	level the lower left cushion let ball disappear into nothingness nafter striking the ball it can be seen at different edge
9	people balls do not stop at the same time it wont let the ball go in the pocket that has hand in it the table control tl
10	the gameplay is fun graphics are good and there are lot of levels however the number of ads are insane is there pai
11	great game until you get above level than it starts shooting balls off screen where can not see them or play anymoi
12	just wanted to thank the supervisors creator those in charge whatever powers that be that after days of my compla
13	as pool player this is good app find it helps me with using different english techniques control of the ball as well as
14	just wanted basic billiards game there was this redundant tutorial level up system that was totally unecessary and
15	installed this game and could not even play it because the game would not load and would shut down waste of tim
16	really enjoyed the older version alot more than now some of these odd ball ntables are more aggravating than enjoy
17	really like the game up to certain point when the normal billiard table is changed to crooked one now its hard to pla
18	pretty decent game but has way too many ads now made me watch second video every time wanted to retry table
19	level and til now no problem but then on this levels the balls keep disappearing under the table and from there there
20	first had trouble getting pass level learned it amp now on level great game finish there are levels total will go back a

Figure 58 Sample screenshot of the clean dataset of after pre-processing

4.16.1.8 Find null entries from the reviews

There appear to be about 700-800 null entries in the dataset review column. Which could occur during the cleaning process to delete null entries with the following commands.

```
<class 'pandas.core.frame.DataFrame'>
Int64Index: 400000 entries, 0 to 399999
Data columns (total 2 columns):
text     399208 non-null object
target 400000 non-null int64
dtypes: int64(1), object (1)
memory usage: 9.2 + MB
```

4.16.1.9 Negative and Positive Words Dictionary

By using the word Cloud Corpus, negative and positive terms are written on the basis of words in a phrase that offer the idea of the form of words in the corpus, as shown in Figure 59.

Positive Word Dictionary   Negitive Word Dictionary

Figure 59 Positive and Negative words dictionary by using the word cloud corpus

4.16.1.10   Semantic analysis of Google play store applications reviews using Logistic Regression Algorithm

This helps you to divide all analysis groups into three separate levels and to test-rate 's faith and see how optimistic, negative and neutral this statement is. Set the goal value to 0 to 1 and test the confidence factor in the ratio and evaluate the analysis class using the logistic regression algorithm, as shown in Figure 60.

1	Reviews	Tags	Confidence	Target
2	wonderfull app completed all levels can not wait for more levels level has bug but you can get around it to complete it by not tou	Positive	0.98	1
3	it good like the gameplay please change up the music as it gets repetitive after the nd level and you can hear the track loop sta	Positive	0.833	1
4	really enjoyed this game until saw one of the adverts throughout the ngame with man and woman spooning it is hardly appropria	Negative	0.997	0
5	please get rid of the odd shaped tables and go back to the classic table please fix level where the balls and cue stick disappear	Negative	0.999	0
6	very easy game to play and has actually given me pointers on how to play nreal game of pool like where to hit the cue ball and	Positive	0.966	1
7	not going to lie just started playing this game probably about hours ago and am thoroughly addicted it pretty awesome game m	Positive	0.956	1
8	level the lower left cushion let ball disappear into nothingness nafter striking the ball it can be seen at different edges of the scre	Neutral	0.546	0
9	people balls do not stop at the same time it wont let the ball go in the pocket that has hand in it the table control the game que	Negative	0.911	1
10	the gameplay is fun graphics are good and there are lot of levels however the number of ads are insane is there paid version whe	Negative	0.687	1
11	great game until you get above level than it starts shooting balls off screen where can not see them or play anymore really have	Negative	0.998	1
12	just wanted to thank the supervisors creator those in charge whatever powers that be that after days of my complaint am no lon	Positive	0.608	1
13	as pool player this is good app find it helps me with using different english techniques control of the ball as well as learning varic	Positive	0.998	1
14	just wanted basic billiards game there was this redundant tutorial level up system that was totally unecessary and map thing to	Negative	1	0
15	installed this game and could not even play it because the game would not load and would shut down waste of time and really v	Negative	0.998	0
16	really enjoyed the older version alot more than now some of these odd ball ntables are more aggravating than enjoyable do not	Negative	0.639	1
17	really like the game up to certain point when the normal billiard table is changed to crooked one now its hard to play the game s	Positive	0.795	1
18	pretty decent game but has way too many ads now made me watch second video every time wanted to retry table no thanks wl	Negative	0.977	1
19	level and til now no problem but then on this levels the balls keep disappearing under the table and from there there no way to w	Negative	0.993	1
20	first had trouble getting pass level learned it amp now on level great game finish there are levels total will go back and replay sor	Negative	0.522	1

Figure 60 Final sentiment analysis results on google play reviews using logistic regression algorithm

4.17 Discussion

More than one million Google Play Store apps can be downloaded from various classified categories. For this research, we have created hundreds and thousands of user app reviews. 148 app reviews were downloaded from 14 categories. Gather from the Google Play Store 506259 reviews. An assessment of the outcomes using an algorithm for master education like Naïve Bayes, Random Forest and Logistic Regression is similarly positive, pessimistic and favorable for semantics in the customer response system. The findings are always optimistic. Calculate the time frequency (TF) and the IDF using specific parameters such as duration, recovery, F1 and the statistical effect. These statistical results are shown in the form of a bar chart. Each algorithm has been analyzed one by one and the results have been contrasted. With hardware such as Random Forest and Naïve Bayes, we have been able to use four separate worrying algorithms with practical regression. Evaluation of Bigram, Trigram and N-gram with different criteria, including precision, recall and F1 ranking, and analysis of the algorithm statistical performance.

The results show that logistic regression is an optimum algorithm for the Google Play Store review. Just before and after the data set has been preprocessed can the logistic regression be provided the optimum convergence speed, aggregation and F1 value. Statistic checking in the TF base since the regression method is preliminarily carried out has an accuracy of 0.622%, an accuracy of 0.414% and repeat of 0.343%, and logistic regression algorithms of 0.621%, an accuracy of 0.404%, a recall of 0.319% and an F1 value of 0.315%. In comparison, after data collection the TF base sport segment has a logistical recording algorithm of 0.623%, a precision of 0.416%, a recall of 0.35% and 0.353% of the F1 score and a TF / IDF logistic decline of 0.629%; a record of 0.331% and F1 of 0.328% and statistically distinct results. In this section the comments were evaluated and classified in positive, pessimistic and neutral words. If the comment rating is optimistic, set the goal rating if a critique is negative, 1 and 0. When the confidence rating falls between 0 and 1 the neutral form will be determined and it should be graded as good.

4.18 Comparison of reviews of rating of Android Apps through sentiment analysis of user comments

4.18.1 Overview

Google Play Store allows users to download an application and provide users with feedback in rates and text reviews. Recent study analyzes that user requirements, user sentiment and experience descriptions are very helpful to an application developer. However, many applications are very extensive and difficult to manually process. The entire program is granted a star rating and the developer cannot evaluate the single function. We scrapped 251661 user reviews through various data scrapping techniques in this research. We have applied different sentimental analysis techniques and check how many positive, negative and natural reviews of an application also, find ranking of applications. We have analyzed the correlation between the average sentiment analysis and average rating of the applications. We have evaluated that most of the application that show the top ranking in the rating graph are not correct in reviews sentiment analysis graph. Because when an uneducated user purchases an android device and download an application from the Google play store. These users do not know the meaning of this star rating and give the 5-star rating after using this application without any understanding about the authentication of the application. We have analyzed that star rating is not authentic in comparison of user reviews because after knowing about the application the users give reviews according to the personal experience.

4.18.2 Sentiment analysis average result of Action Category

We have scrapped the user reviews and app rating of top 6 applications of action category from Google play store. The statistical information of rating and reviews are shown in Table 20. In the rating graph of Figure 61, we have compared these results by seeing the graph of rating is respectively talking tom gold run, Warship battle, Bus Rush, Real Gangster crime, zombie frontier 3 and metal soldiers. In the review's sentiment graph of Figure 61, we have analyzed that Bus rush application is at the first number, which was the third number in rating graph. The zombie frontier 3 is a second number application in review graph, which was at the fifth number in the rating graph. The talking tom gold run is third number application in review graph, which was at first number in rating graph. The warship battle is the fourth number application in review graph, which was at second number in rating graph. The real gangster is the fifth number application in review graph, which was at the fourth number in the rating graph. The metal soldier is the sixth number application in review graph, which was at the same as the sixth number of rating graph. We have evaluated that most of the application that show the top ranking in the rating graph are not correct in reviews sentiment analysis graph. Because when an uneducated user purchases an android device and download an application from the Google play store. The application shows the rating star, and these users do not know the meaning of this rating star and give the 5-star rating after using this application without any understanding about the authentication of the application. We have analyzed that star rating is not authentic user reviews because when a user gives a review, the first user uses the application, and after knowing about the application the give reviews according to the personal experience.

Table 20 Statistical information of Sentiment analysis average result of Action Category

Application Name	Reviews sentiment average						Rating sentiment average					
	Bus Rush	Metal Soldiers	Real Gangster Crime	Talking Tom Gold Run	WARSHIP BATTLE	Zombie Frontier 3	Bus Rush	Metal Soldiers	Real Gangster Crime	Talking Tom Gold Run	WARSHIP BATTLE	Zombie Frontier 3
	1.297	0.567	0.569	1.102	0.911	1.109	4.2385	3.6316	4.0586	4.7127	4.2255	3.8082

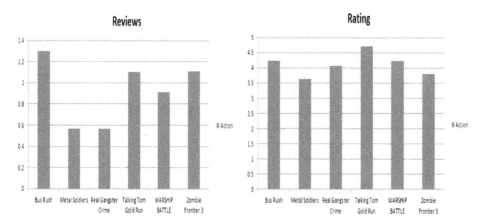

Figure 61 Final sentiment analysis results on google play reviews using logistic regression algorithm

4.18.3 Sentiment analysis average result of Art & Design Category

We have scrapped the user reviews and app rating of top 8 applications of art and design category from Google play store. The statistical information of rating and reviews are shown in Table 21. In the rating graph of Figure 62, we have compared these results by seeing the graph of rating that is U Launcher Lite-FREE Live Cool Themes, Hide Apps application are at first number, Canvas application is at second number, Sketch - Draw & Paint is at third, PaperColor is at fourth number, ibis Paint X and TextArt Cool

Text creator are at fifth number, MediBang Paint - Make Art is at sixth number and ArtFlow Paint Draw Sketchbook is at seventh number. In the review's sentiment graph of Figure 62, we have analyzed that Canvas application is at the first number, which was at the second number in rating graph. The TextArt Cool Text creator is a second number application in review graph, which was at the fourth number in the rating graph. The ArtFlow Paint Draw Sketchbook is third number application in review graph, which was at sixth number in rating graph. The ibis Paint X is the fourth number application in review graph, which was at fourth number in rating graph.

The PaperColor is the fifth number application in review graph, which was at the third number in the rating graph. The MediBang Paint - Make Art is the sixth number application in review graph, which was at fifth number of rating graph. The Sketch - Draw & Paint is the seventh number application in review graph, which was at fifth number of rating graph. The U Launcher Lite-FREE Live Cool Themes, Hide Apps is the eighth number application in review graph, which was at first number of rating graph. We have evaluated that most of the application that show the top ranking in the rating graph are not correct in reviews sentiment analysis graph. Because when an uneducated user purchases an android device and download an application from the Google play store. The application shows the rating star, and these users do not know the meaning of this rating star and give the 5-star rating after using this application without any understanding about the authentication of the application. We have analyzed that star rating is not authentic user reviews because when a user gives a review, the first user uses the application, and after knowing about the application the give reviews according to the personal experience.

Table 21 Statistical information of Sentiment analysis average result of art & design Category

Application Name	Reviews sentiment average								Rating sentiment average							
	ArtFlow Paint Draw Sketchbook	Canvas	ibis Paint X	MediBang Paint - Make Art	PaperColor	Sketch - Draw & Paint	TextArt Cool Text creator	U Launcher Lite-FREE Live Cool Themes, Hide Apps	ArtFlow Paint Draw Sketchbook	Canvas	ibis Paint X	MediBang Paint - Make Art	PaperColor	Sketch - Draw & Paint	TextArt Cool Text creator	U Launcher Lite -FREE Live Cool Themes, Hide Apps
	2.272	2.732	2.246	2.033	2.179	1.974	2.354	1.076	4.119	4.688 7	4.335	4.297 7	4.385 5	4.391 5	4.335	4.690 7

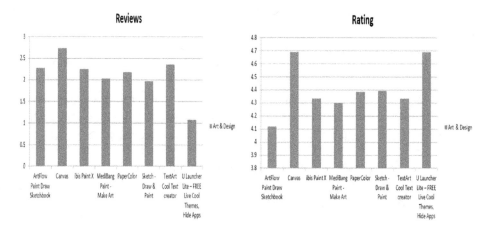

Figure 62 Bar chart visualization of reviews and rating of Sentiment analysis average result of Art & Design Category

4.18.4 Sentiment analysis average result of Casual Category

We have scrapped the user reviews and app rating of top 10 applications of casual category from Google play store. The statistical information of rating and reviews are shown in Table 22. In the rating graph of Figure 63, we have compared these results by seeing the graph of rating that is Farm Heroes Super Saga application are at first number, Candy Crush Saga application is at second number, Angry Birds POP Bubble

Shooter is at third, Hay Day is at fourth number, My Talking Tom is at fifth number, Gardenscapes is at sixth number, Pou is at seventh number, Bubble Shooter is at eighth number, Minion Rush Despicable Me Official Game is at ninth number and Board Kings is at tenth number. In the review's sentiment graph of Figure 63, we have analyzed that My Talking Tom application is at the first number, which was at the fifth number in rating graph. The Pou is a second number application in review graph, which was at the seventh number in the rating graph.

The Minion Rush Despicable Me Official Game is third number application in review graph, which was at ninth number in rating graph. The Farm Heroes Super Saga is the fourth number application in review graph, which was at first number in rating graph. The Candy Crush Saga is the fifth number application in review graph, which was at the second number in the rating graph. The Board Kings is the sixth number application in review graph, which was at tenth number of rating graph. The Gardenscapes is the seventh number application in review graph, which was at sixth number of rating graph. The Bubble Shooter is the eighth number application in review graph, which was at eighth number of rating graph. The Hay Day is the ninth number application in review graph, which was at fourth number of rating graph. The Angry Birds POP Bubble Shooter is the tenth number application in review graph, which was at third number of rating graph. We have evaluated that most of the application that show the top ranking in the rating graph are not correct in reviews sentiment analysis graph. Because when an uneducated user purchases an android device and download an application from the Google play store. The application shows the rating star, and these users do not know the meaning of this rating star and give the 5-star rating after using this application without any understanding about the authentication of the application.

Table 22 Statistical information of Sentiment analysis average result of casual Category

Application Name	Reviews sentiment average										Rating sentiment average									
	Angry Birds POP Bubble Shooter	Board Kings	Bubble Shooter	Candy Crush Saga	Farm Heroes Super Saga	Gardenscapes	Hay Day	Minion Rush Despicable Me Official	My Talking Tom	Pou	Angry Birds POP Bubble Shooter	Board Kings	Bubble Shooter	Candy Crush Saga	Farm Heroes Super Saga	Gardenscapes	Hay Day	Minion Rush Despicable Me Official Game	My Talking Tom	Pou
	0.875	1.232	1.029	1.338	1.358	1.140	0.946	1.521	1.935	1.814	4.5666	4.2024	4.4040	4.5681	4.6205	4.5083	4.5432	4.2510	4.5343	4.4633

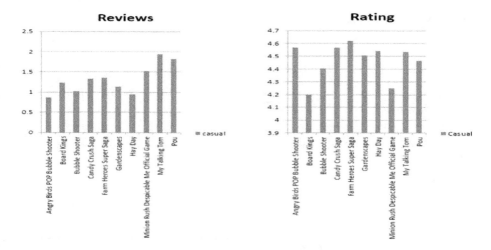

Figure 63 Bar chart visualization of reviews and rating of Sentiment analysis average result of Casual Category

4.18.5 Sentiment analysis average result of Communication Category

We have scrapped the user reviews and app rating of top 10 applications of communication category from Google play store. The statistical information of rating and reviews are shown in Table 23. In the rating graph of Figure 64, we have compared these results by seeing the graph of rating that is Opera Mini browser beta application is at first number, Google Duo application is at second number, UC Browser Mini is at third, Messenger Lite is at fourth number, Firefox Browser is at fifth number, KakaoTalk is at sixth number, Hangouts Dialer is at seventh number, Line is at eighth number, WeChat is at ninth number and Dolphin Browser is at tenth number. In the review's sentiment graph of Figure 64, we have analyzed that Google Duo is at the first number, which was at the second number in rating graph. The KakaoTalk is a second number application in review graph, which was at the sixth number in the rating graph. The Opera Mini browser beta is third number application in review graph, which was at first number in rating graph. The Hangouts Dialer is the fourth number application in review graph, which was at seventh number in rating graph. The Dolphin Browser is the fifth number application in review graph, which was at the tenth number in the rating graph. The Firefox Browser is the sixth number application in review graph, which was at fifth number of rating graph. The Messenger Lite is the seventh number application in review graph, which was at fourth number of rating graph. The UC Browser Mini is the eighth number application in review graph, which was at third number of rating graph. The Line is the ninth number application in review graph, which was at eighth number of rating graph. The WeChat is the tenth number application in review graph, which was at ninth number of rating graph. We have evaluated that most of the application that show the top ranking in the rating graph are not correct in reviews sentiment analysis graph. Because when an uneducated user purchases an android device and download an application from the Google play store. The application shows the rating star, and these users do not know the meaning of this rating star and give the 5-star rating after using this application without any understanding about the authentication of the application. We have analyzed that star rating is not authentic user reviews because when a user gives a review, the first user uses the application, and after knowing about the application the give reviews according to the personal experience.

Table 23 Statistical information of Sentiment analysis average result of Communication Category

Application Name	Reviews sentiment average										Rating sentiment average									
	Dolphin Browser	Firefox Browser	Google Duo	Hangouts Dialer	KakaoTalk	LINE	Messenger Lite	Opera Mini browser beta	UC Browser Mini	WeChat	Dolphin Browser	Firefox Browser	Google Duo	Hangouts Dialer	KakaoTalk	LINE	Messenger Lite	Opera Mini browser beta	UC Browser Mini	WeChat
	1.56	1.45	2.56	1.68	1.82	0.80	1.39	1.72	1.13	0.63	2.75	4.12	4.46	3.22	3.72	3.12	4.18	4.62	4.20	2.92

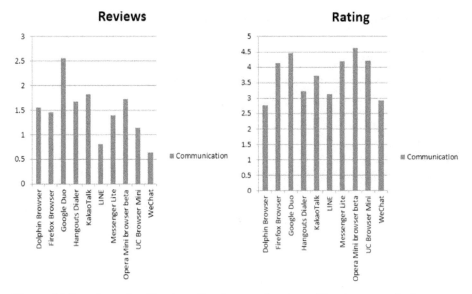

Figure 64 Bar chart visualization of reviews and rating of Sentiment analysis average result of Communication Category

4.18.6 Sentiment analysis average result of Health & Fitness Category

We have scrapped the user reviews and app rating of top 4 applications of health & fitness category from Google play store. The statistical information of rating and reviews are shown in Table 24. In the rating graph of Figure 65, we have compared these results by seeing the graph of rating that is Lose Belly Fat in 30 Days - Flat Stomach application is at first number, Home Workout - No Equipment application is at second number, Lose Weight in 30 Days is at third and Water Drink Reminder is at fourth number. In the review's sentiment graph of Figure 65, we have analyzed that Lose Belly Fat in 30 Days - Flat Stomach, Home Workout-No Equipment, Lose Weight in 30 Days and Water Drink Reminder are at the same level of review graph as in rating graph.

Table 24 Statistical information of Sentiment analysis average result of health &
fitness Category

Application Name	Reviews sentiment average				Rating sentiment average			
	Home Workout - No Equipment	Lose Belly Fat in 30 Days - Flat Stomach	Lose Weight in 30 Days	Water Drink Reminder	Home Workout - No Equipment	Lose Belly Fat in 30 Days - Flat Stomach	Lose Weight in 30 Days	Water Drink Reminder
	2.509	2.680	2.413	2.361	4.8240	4.8986	4.8153	4.8003

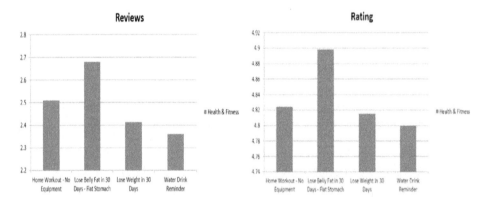

Figure 65 Bar chart visualization of reviews and rating of Sentiment analysis average
result of Health & Fitness Category

4.18.7 Sentiment analysis average result of Photography Category

We have scrapped the user reviews and app rating of top 7 applications of photography category from Google play store. The statistical information of rating and reviews are shown in Table 25. In the rating graph of Figure 66, we have compared these results by seeing the graph of rating that is BeautyPlus is at first number, Sweet Snap application is at second number, Music Video Maker is at third, HDCamera is at fourth number, BeautyCam is at fifth number, B612-Beauty & Filter Camera is at sixth number and Motorola Camera is at seventh number. In the review's sentiment graph of Figure 66, we have analyzed that Music Video Maker is at the first number, which was at the third number in rating graph. The BeautyCam is a second number application in review graph, which was at the fifth number in the rating graph. The B612-Beauty & Filter Camera is third number application in review graph, which was at sixth number in rating graph. The Sweet Snap is the fourth number application in review graph, which was at second number in rating graph. The BeautyPlus is the fifth number application in review graph, which was at the first number in the rating graph.

The HDCamera is the sixth number application in review graph, which was at fourth number of rating graph. The Motorola Camera is the seventh number application in review graph, which was same as rating graph. We have evaluated that most of the application that show the top ranking in the rating graph are not correct in reviews sentiment analysis graph. Because when an uneducated user purchases an android device and download an application from the Google play store. The application shows the rating star, and these users do not know the meaning of this rating star and give the 5-star rating after using this application without any understanding about the authentication of the application. We have analyzed that star rating is not authentic user reviews because when a user gives a review, the first user uses the application, and after knowing about the application the give reviews according to the personal experience.

Table 25 Statistical information of Sentiment analysis average result of photography Category

Application Name	Reviews sentiment average							Rating sentiment average						
	B612 - Beauty & Filter Camera	BeautyCam	BeautyPlus	HDCamera	Motorola Camera	Music Video Maker	Sweet Snap	B612 - Beauty & Filter Camera	BeautyCam	BeautyPlus	HDCamera	Motorola Camera	Music Video Maker	Sweet Snap
	1.695	2.012	1.567	1.514	0.747	2.242	1.633	4.2375	4.3975	4.6475	4.4107	2.3131	4.6092	4.6241

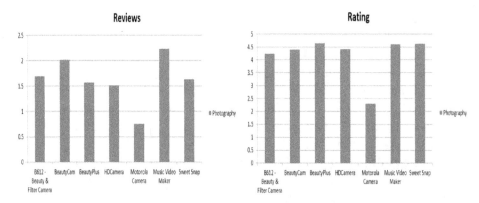

Figure 66 Bar chart visualization of reviews and rating of Sentiment analysis average result of Photography Category

4.18.8 Sentiment analysis average result of Racing Category

We have scrapped the user reviews and app rating of top 8 applications of racing category from Google play store. The statistical information of rating and reviews are shown in Table 26. In the rating graph of Figure 67, we have compared these results by seeing the graph of rating is respectively Beach Buggy Racing, Racing Fever Moto, Bike Mayhem Free, Dr. Driving 2, Asphalt Nitro, Trial Xtreme 4, Extreme Car Driving Simulator and Racing in Car 2. In the review's sentiment graph of Figure 67, we have analyzed that Dr. Driving 2 is at the first number, which was at the fourth number in rating graph. The Asphalt Nitro is a second number application in review graph, which was at the fifth number in the rating graph. The Racing Fever Moto is third number application in review graph, which was at second number in rating graph. The Extreme Car Driving Simulator is the fourth number application in review graph, which was at seventh number in rating graph.

The Beach Buggy Racing is the fifth number application in review graph, which was at the first number in the rating graph. The Bike Mayhem Free is the sixth number application in review graph, which was at third number of rating graph. The Trial Xtreme 4 is the seventh number application in review graph, which at sixth number of rating graph. The Racing in Car 2 is the eighth number application in review graph, which was same as in rating graph. We have evaluated that most of the application that show the top ranking in the rating graph are not correct in reviews sentiment analysis graph. Because when an uneducated user purchases an android device and download an application from the Google play store. The application shows the rating star, and these users do not know the meaning of this rating star and give the 5-star rating after using this application without any understanding about the authentication of the application. We have analyzed that star rating is not authentic user reviews because when a user gives a review, the first user uses the application, and after knowing about the application the give reviews according to the personal experience.

Table 26 Statistical information of Sentiment analysis average result of racing Category

	Sentiment analysis average result of Racing Category															
	Reviews sentiment average								Rating sentiment average							
Application Name	Asphalt Nitro	Beach Buggy Racing	Bike Mayhem Free	Dr. Driving 2	Extreme Car Driving Simulator	Racing Fever Moto	Racing in Car 2	Trial Xtreme 4	Asphalt Nitro	Beach Buggy Racing	Bike Mayhem Free	Dr. Driving 2	Extreme Car Driving Simulator	Racing Fever Moto	Racing in Car 2	Trial Xtreme 4
	1.282	1.034	0.887	1.329	1.095	1.113	0.382	0.677	4.4445	4.6206	4.5320	4.4877	4.3401	4.5527	3.8731	4.3538

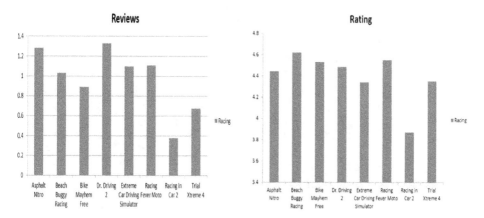

Figure 67 Bar chart visualization of reviews and rating of Sentiment analysis average result of Racing Category

4.18.9 Sentiment analysis average result of Shopping Category

We have scrapped the user reviews and app rating of top 8 applications of shopping category from Google play store. The statistical information of rating and reviews are shown in Table 27. In the rating graph of Figure 68, we have compared these results by seeing the graph of rating is respectively Lazada, AliExpress, Bikro, Myntra Online Shopping App, Flipkart Online Shopping App, ShopClues Online Shopping App,

Snapdeal Online Shopping App and Amazon for Tablets. In the review's sentiment graph of Figure 68, we have analyzed that Bikro is at the first number, which was at the third number in rating graph. The AliExpress is a second number application in review graph, which was same as in the rating graph.

The Lazada is third number application in review graph, which was at first number in rating graph. The Myntra Online Shopping App is the fourth number application in review graph, which was same as in rating graph. The Flipkart Online Shopping App is the fifth number application in review graph, which was same as in the rating graph. The ShopClues Online Shopping App is the sixth number application in review graph, which was same as in rating graph. The TAmazon for Tablets is the seventh number application in review graph, which was at eighth number of rating graph. The Snapdeal Online Shopping App is the eighth number application in review graph, which was at seventh number of rating graph. We have evaluated that most of the application that show the top ranking in the rating graph are not correct in reviews sentiment analysis graph. Because when an uneducated user purchases an android device and download an application from the Google play store. The application shows the rating star, and these users do not know the meaning of this rating star and give the 5-star rating after using this application without any understanding about the authentication of the application. We have analyzed that star rating is not authentic user reviews because when a user gives a review, the first user uses the application, and after knowing about the application the give reviews according to the personal experience.

Table 27 Statistical information of Sentiment analysis average result of shopping Category

Application Name	Sentiment analysis average result of Shopping Category															
	Reviews sentiment average								Rating sentiment average							
	AliExpress	Amazon for Tablets	Bikroy	Flipkart Online Shopping App	Lazada	Myntra Online Shopping App	ShopClues Online Shopping App	Snapdeal Online Shopping App	AliExpress	Amazon for Tablets	Bikroy	Flipkart Online Shopping App	Lazada	Myntra Online Shopping App	ShopClues Online Shopping App	Snapdeal Online Shopping App
	1.720	1.181	1.805	1.441	1.600	1.559	1.211	0.808	4.5408	3.2733	4.4964	3.8021	4.5925	3.9335	3.5867	3.2905

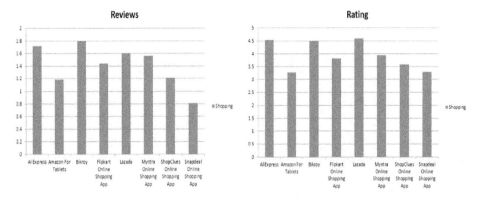

Figure 68 Bar chart visualization of reviews and rating of Sentiment analysis average result of Shopping Category

4.18.10   Sentiment analysis average result of Sports Category

We have scrapped the user reviews and app rating of top 6 applications of sports category from Google play store. The statistical information of rating and reviews are shown in Table 28. In the rating graph of Figure 69, we have compared these results by seeing the graph of rating is respectively Score! Hero, Tennis, FVolleyball Champions 3, Real Cricket™ 18, Table Tennis3D and Real Football. In the review's sentiment graph of Figure 69, we have analyzed that FVolleyball Champions 3 is at the first number, which was at the third number in rating graph.

The Real Cricket™ 18 is a second number application in review graph, which was at fourth number in the rating graph. The Tennis is third number application in review graph, which was at second number in rating graph. The Table Tennis3D is the fourth number application in review graph, which was at fifth number in rating graph. The Score! Hero is the fifth number application in review graph, which was at first number in rating graph. The Real Football is the sixth number application in review graph, which was same as in rating graph. We have evaluated that most of the application that show the top ranking in the rating graph are not correct in reviews sentiment analysis graph. Because when an uneducated user purchases an android device and download an application from the Google play store. The application shows the rating star, and these users do not know the meaning of this rating star and give the 5-star rating after using this application without any understanding about the authentication of the application.

Table 28 Statistical information of Sentiment analysis average result of sports Category

Application Name	Sentiment analysis average result of Sports Category											
	Reviews sentiment average						Rating sentiment average					
	FVolleyball Champions 3D	Real Cricket™ 18	Real Football	Score! Hero	Table Tennis 3D	Tennis	FVolleyball Champions 3D	Real Cricket™ 18	Real Football	Score! Hero	Table Tennis 3D	Tennis
	1.443	1.339	0.788	0.835	0.939	1.118	4.1341	4.003	3.7315	4.3879	3.8313	4.309

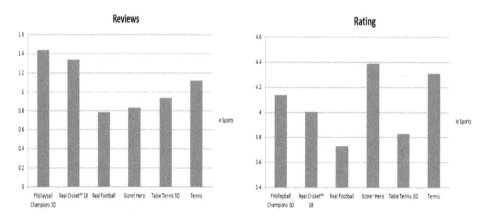

Figure 69 Bar chart visualization of reviews and rating of Sentiment analysis average result of Sports Category

4.19 Correlation Coefficient

We have calculated the correlation between application rating and sentiment analysis of reviews. We show the graph of correlation. Correlation is the relationship between two or more than variables. The value of correlation lies between -1 to 1. If our answer is not in range, then our answer is wrong. So, correlation 0 means no correlation and if correlation is -1 that it is perfect negative correlation, if correlation is +1 that means perfect positive correlation and if correlation is lies between 0 to -1 and 0 to +1 that means higher degree of correlation.

4.19.1 Positive Correlation

It is a situation that if one variable is increase that second variable also increase and if one variable is decrease then second variable also decrease. That is a positive correlation.

4.19.2 Negative Correlation

It is a situation that if one variable is increase that second variable is decrease and if one variable is decrease then second variable also increase. That is a Negative correlation.

4.19.3 No Correlation

No correlation means that there is no positive or negative increase for every increase. Two are not just related Figure 70.

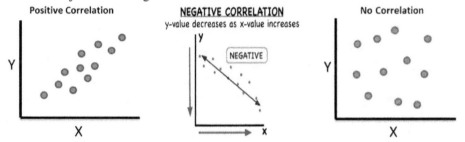

Figure 70 Graph representation of positive, Negative and No correlation

4.19.4 Pearson Correlation Coefficient

The following is a formula for the person correlation coefficient r.

$$r = \frac{\sum XY - \frac{(\sum X)(\sum Y)}{n}}{\sqrt{\left(\sum X^2 - \frac{(\sum X)^2}{n}\right)\left(\sum Y^2 - \frac{(\sum Y)^2}{n}\right)}}$$

Now we will solve the formula for this numerical.

X	Y
1	2
3	5
4	5
4	8

$$\sum XY = (1)(2) + (3)(5) + (4)(5) + (4)(8) = 69$$

$$\sum X = 1 + 3 + 4 + 4 = 12$$

$$\sum Y = 2 + 5 + 5 + 8 = 2$$

$$\sum X^2 = 1^2 + 3^2 + 4^2 + 4^2 = 42$$

$$\sum Y^2 = 2^2 + 5^2 + 5^2 + 8^2 = 118$$

$$r = \frac{69 - \frac{(12)(20)}{4}}{\sqrt{\left(42 - \frac{(12)^2}{4}\right)\left(118 - \frac{(20)^2}{4}\right)}} = .866$$

4.19.5 Results of the correlation of the average of sentiment analysis and rating.

Complete processing of all the data we get some results. First, we get the result in the form of graph that how people are reacting on Ali Baba Express by sentiment analyzing 1000 user reviews. We get the pie graph of every application, but we show as a sample graph of one application. In this we show that 1000 comments fetch this application that name is Ali Baba Express. It is a shopping Application. Inside it first we find the sentiment analysis of reviews and show graph of the sentiment analysis of reviews. That show in 1000 comments there are 62.90% positive comments 14.40% neutral comments and 22.70% negative comments on this application. In the Second number we get the ranking result as shown in Figure 71.

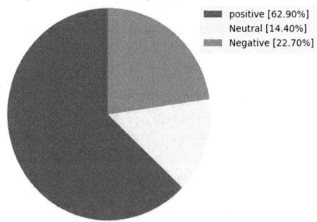

Figure 71 The percentage of positive, negative or neutral reviews

First, we show the application name, second average rating, third average sentiment analysis of reviews and last show the correlation between average rating and average sentiment analysis of reviews that can shown in Figure 72.

🎮 tk

Application Name = Media Player Average Rating = 3.351 Average Sentiment Analysis = 2.09 Correlation = 0.509205905765691
Application Name = GOM Player Average Rating = 3.723 Average Sentiment Analysis = 2.44 Correlation = 0.427654826781813
Application Name = VLC Player Average Rating = 3.925 Average Sentiment Analysis = 2.61 Correlation = 0.432996768394113
Application Name = MX Player Average Rating = 4.067 Average Sentiment Analysis = 3.23 Correlation = 0.417805181528597
Application Name = Music Player Average Rating = 4.573 Average Sentiment Analysis = 4.78 Correlation = 0.192625652278267

Figure 72 Statistical information of different parameters of Android Application

Inside it we sort the values. In the third number we get the correlation graph that can show in Figure 73.

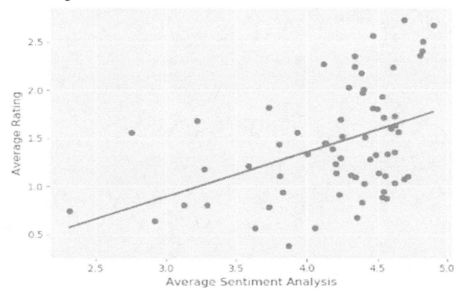

Figure 73 Correlation coefficient representation of average sentiment analysis and average rating

4.20 Discussion

User can download and use these applications, and give an evaluation on the application's experience in the form of comments or reviews, on a scale of 0-5. In this work, we have scrapped 251661 user reviews by various techniques for scraping data. in evaluated result of this research we have applied text classification on our dataset after preprocessing. After comparison of the different attributes we have found the best algorithm which have the best accuracy. We have applied different sentimental analysis techniques and check how many positive, negative and natural reviews of an application also, find ranking of applications. We have analyzed the correlation between the average sentiment analysis and average rating of the applications. We have evaluated that most of the application that show the top ranking in the rating graph are not correct in reviews sentiment analysis graph. Because when an uneducated user purchases an android device and download an application from the Google play store. These users do not know the meaning of this star rating and give the 5-star rating after using this application without any understanding about the authentication of the application. We have analyzed that star rating is not authentic in comparison of user reviews because after knowing about the application the users give reviews according to the personal experience.

5   CONCLUSION AND FUTURE WORK

5.1   Conclusion

Thousands of developers and users come to GP store to upload and download apps. Such apps also include sports, entertainment, videos, etc. All apps uploaded to a play store always have two main types, free and paid. We have scrapped 550 applications of every free and paying type of games in this research report. We have a 10k application free and 3600 paying programs for various types of games in the final analysis of the data collection. Adventure, Arcade, Casino, Casual, Card, Educational, Music, Puzzle, Racing, Role Playing, Sports, Strategy, Simulation, Trivia, Word are the categories for this application. We also scraped 70 separate attributes with each program, but in this study, we are utilizing four review attributes, namely scores, IAP, Advertisements and Installs. In order to evaluate attributes and test associations between various attributes, the RStudio and the CIRCOS method are used. CIRCOS verifies the multiple configurations with comparative details on specific collections, such as percentiles, elements and colors.

LSA of online reviews of the user to the game application, this research is recognized and compared determinants of positive and negative behavior in the direction of large/arena games/big application/enterprise app, mini-games/small application. Toward of each Type of Games the main conclusion is the following: According to the first question of research, a research found that for each kind of game application, user positive and negative behavior determinants were diverse. Moderately, the determinants of user positiveness were more frequent and explained the center of applications. These determinants integrated as Game enjoyment, Effort for gameplay, Game recommendation, Offers in games and Graphics. Additionally, the determinants of user negativeness were more precise, including less Game Enjoyment, Gameplay, Game Recommendation, and Advertisement. Moreover, the research found that for every kind of game application, number of user's negativeness factors was higher than the number of user positiveness element, which explained that the cause of negativeness was more significant than the cause of positiveness for users staying in every kind of game application. According to the second question of research, the research found that for every kind of game application, determinants of user positive and negative behavior were not uniformly significant. Rankings of the significance can be rank for each factor that led to user positiveness, or negativeness were prearranged according to the singular values in Table 4 - Table 7.

According to the third question of research, the research found that type of determinants for user's positiveness was approximately similar for every kind of game application; these determinants had different raking of importance.

123

The game recommendation was the most influential factor in determining user positiveness towards for large/arena games/big application/enterprise app, mini-games/small application, and towards Each Type of Games. Game enjoyment can play a most manipulating role in user positiveness toward large/arena games/big application/enterprise app and mini games/small application. Then, the research recognized an extra determinant of user positiveness toward each type of game application. Gameplay was imperative for users of large/arena games/big application/enterprise app, mini-games/small application, and towards Each Type of Games. A Graphics was necessary for large/arena games/big application/enterprise app, mini-games/small application users. For each determinant of user negativeness, the research found both kind and the rankings were dissimilar between diverse types of game applications. Amongst the diverse factors recognized as determinants of negativeness, Game Enjoyment, Gameplay, Game Recommendation, Advertisement, In-app-purchase and Waiting for rejoin the game (Online game) created the most significant amount of negativeness among users of large/arena games/big application/enterprise app, mini-games/small application and towards Each Type of Games.

More than one million Google Play Store apps can be downloaded from various classified categories. For this research, we have created hundreds and thousands of user app reviews. 148 app reviews were downloaded from 14 categories. Gather from the Google Play Store 506259 reviews. Evaluation of Bigram, Trigram and N-gram with different criteria, including precision, recall and F1 ranking, and analysis of the algorithm statistical performance. An assessment of the outcome using a particular algorithm in machine learning, such as Naïve Bayes, Random Forest and the Logistic Regression method, is similarly optimistic, negative and neutral for the semantics in the program consumer feedback. Calculate time-frequency (TF) and IDF by using various parameters such as accuracy, recall, F1 and the statistical effect of these calculations. In the shape of a bar map, display such statistical findings. The analysis of each algorithm was carried out one by one and the findings were contrasted. The results evaluated show that logistic regression could be an optimal algorithm for reviewing this Google Play Store tool. The logistic regression is given the optimal speed of convergence, collection, and F1 value only before and after their data set has been preprocessed. Statistic checking in the TF base since the regression method is preliminarily carried out has an accuracy of 0.622%, an accuracy of 0.414% and repeat of 0.343%, and logistic regression algorithms of 0.621%, an accuracy of 0.404%, a recall of 0.319% and an F1 value of 0.315%. In comparison, after data collection the TF base sport segment has a logistical recording algorithm of 0.623%, a precision of 0.416%, a recall of 0.35% and 0.353% of the F1 score and a TF / IDF logistic decline of 0.629%; a record of 0.331% and F1 of 0.328% and statistically distinct results. In this section the comments were evaluated and classified in positive, pessimistic and neutral words. If the comment rating is optimistic, set the goal rating if a critique is negative, 1 and 0. When the confidence rating falls between 0 and 1 the neutral form will be determined and it should be graded as good.

The main platform for accessing and uploading the Android version was today Google Play Store. This app is used by Android users for personal use. Through program consumer has a customer history. These applications can be downloaded and utilized by users and the application may be assessed on an experience level from 0-5 in the form of comments or reviews. In this work, we have scrapped 251661 user reviews by various techniques for scraping data. We applied a text classification to our data collection after preprocessing in the analyzed results of this study. We also used various algorithms to know the exactness, precision, recall and F1 performance. Upon evaluating the numerous parameters, we find the most reliable algorithm. We also implemented numerous emotional analysis strategies and test how many optimistic, negative and normal evaluations an application gets, too. The connection between the average opinion study and the average product ranking has been evaluated. We also determined that most applications with the highest grade in the table are not right in the opinion analysis sample of ratings. That when an uneducated person buys an android smartphone and runs a Google play store program. These users do not recognize the significance of this star rating and, after utilizing this program, offer the 5-star rating without any knowledge of the device authentication. We have analyzed that star ratings are not authentic compared to user reviews because users provide reviews based on personal experience, after knowing the application.

5.2 Future Work

Throughout future research, we will test the correlations of numerous programs. To find the connections between specific attributes, we must build clusters with various attributes. We may use these data to measure and analyze GP storage applications accurately.

This research can be extended as follows by researchers of the future. Firstly, this research compares positive and negative user behavior determinants from various types of game applications. In future studies, the determinants of positive and negative user behavior can be compared from the perspective of user demographics. For example, future studies can investigate whether the user's age, the gender of the user or the reason of the game can influence their positive and negative behavior towards a game application. Secondly, the impact of electronic word of mouth can be recognized among a range of demographic groups of users and game types. For e.g., which category or form of consumer demographic activity is more affected by a positive electronic word of mouth and which demographic group or type of game are most harmed by an electronic word of mouth? A question like, Will the game developer press eWOM online reaction and communication? Ultimately, however, encouraging the matching feature in the app could improve user positivity and alleviate user negativity, thus increasing demand and the cost of services cannot be ignored.

Increase the category of applications and the number of exams. Compare the findings with certain implementations with the logistic regression method. Generate clusters and check the link between evaluation and application ratings, allowing each application to be analyzed more closely.

REFERENCES

AGGARWAL, C. C. & ZHAI, C. 2012. *Mining text data*, Springer Science & Business Media.

AL-SUBAIHIN, A., FINKELSTEIN, A., HARMAN, M., JIA, Y., MARTIN, W., SARRO, F. & ZHANG, Y. App store mining and analysis. Proceedings of the 3rd International Workshop on Software Development Lifecycle for Mobile, 2015. ACM, 1-2.

ALDABBAS, H., BAJAHZAR, A., ALRUILY, M., QURESHI, A. A., LATIF, R. M. A. & FARHAN, M. 2020. Google Play Content Scraping and Knowledge Engineering using Natural Language Processing Techniques with the Analysis of User Reviews. *Journal of Intelligent Systems, 30,* 192-208.

ARAQUE, O., ZHU, G. & IGLESIAS, C. A. 2019. A semantic similarity-based perspective of affect lexicons for sentiment analysis. *Knowledge-Based Systems,* 165, 346-359.

AROGUNDADE, O., ABAYOMI-ALLI, A., FATOYE, I., ADEJUYIGBE, C. & OLOWE, V. 2019. Development of an Android Based Mobile Application for the Production and Management of Organic Manure (MoAPOM). *Journal of Organic Agriculture and Environment,* 6.

ATKINSON, J., FERREIRA, A. & ARAVENA, E. Discovering implicit intention-level knowledge from natural-language texts. International Conference on Innovative Techniques and Applications of Artificial Intelligence, 2008. Springer, 249-262.

BAGNASCO, S., BERZANO, D., GUARISE, A., LUSSO, S., MASERA, M. & VALLERO, S. Monitoring of IaaS and scientific applications on the Cloud using the Elasticsearch ecosystem. Journal of physics: Conference series, 2015. IOP Publishing, 012016.

BUSINGE, J., OPENJA, M., KAVALER, D., BAINOMUGISHA, E., KHOMH, F. & FILKOV, V. Studying android app popularity by cross-linking github and google play store. 2019 IEEE 26th International Conference on Software Analysis, Evolution and Reengineering (SANER), 2019. IEEE, 287-297.

CHEN, J., HUANG, H., TIAN, S. & QU, Y. J. E. S. W. A. 2009. Feature selection for text classification with Naïve Bayes. 36, 5432-5435.

CHEN, K., WANG, P., LEE, Y., WANG, X., ZHANG, N., HUANG, H., ZOU, W. & LIU, P. Finding Unknown Malice in 10 Seconds: Mass Vetting for New Threats at the Google-Play Scale. USENIX Security Symposium, 2015.

CHERKASSKY, V. & MA, Y. J. N. N. 2004. Practical selection of SVM parameters and noise estimation for SVM regression. 17, 113-126.

CIURUMELEA, A., PANICHELLA, S. & GALL, H. C. Automated user reviews analyser. Proceedings of the 40th International Conference on Software Engineering: Companion Proceeedings, 2018. ACM, 317-318.

CRUSSELL, J., GIBLER, C. & CHEN, H. Attack of the clones: Detecting cloned applications on android markets. European Symposium on Research in Computer Security, 2012. Springer, 37-54.

DAY, M.-Y. & LIN, Y.-D. Deep Learning for Sentiment Analysis on Google Play Consumer Review. Information Reuse and Integration (IRI), 2017 IEEE International Conference on, 2017. IEEE, 382-388.

DEO, A., DASH, S. K., SUAREZ-TANGIL, G., VOVK, V. & CAVALLARO, L. Prescience: Probabilistic guidance on the retraining conundrum for malware detection. Proceedings of the 2016 ACM Workshop on Artificial Intelligence and Security, 2016. ACM, 71-82.

DI SORBO, A., PANICHELLA, S., ALEXANDRU, C. V., SHIMAGAKI, J., VISAGGIO, C. A., CANFORA, G. & GALL, H. C. What would users change in my app? summarizing app reviews for recommending software changes. Proceedings of the 2016 24th ACM SIGSOFT International Symposium on Foundations of Software Engineering, 2016. ACM, 499-510.

FAN, Z. 2019. Tweet analysis for Android malware detection in Google Play Store.

GENC-NAYEBI, N. & ABRAN, A. 2017. A systematic literature review: Opinion mining studies from mobile app store user reviews. *Journal of Systems and Software,* 125, 207-219.

GEORGIEV, G. V. & GEORGIEV, D. D. 2018. Enhancing user creativity: Semantic measures for idea generation. *Knowledge-Based Systems,* 151, 1-15.

GOLDBERG, Y. 2017. Neural network methods for natural language processing. *Synthesis Lectures on Human Language Technologies,* 10, 1-309.

GOMEZ, M. 2016. *Towards Improving the Quality of Mobile Apps by Leveraging Crowdsourced Feedback.* Universite Lille 1; Inria Lille-Nord Europe.

GÓMEZ, M., ROUVOY, R., MONPERRUS, M. & SEINTURIER, L. A recommender system of buggy app checkers for app store moderators. Proceedings of the Second ACM International Conference on Mobile Software Engineering and Systems, 2015. IEEE Press, 1-11.

GROENEWEGEN, M., STOYANOV, D., DEICHMANN, D. & VAN HALTEREN, A. Connecting with active people matters: the influence of an online community on physical activity behavior. International Conference on Social Informatics, 2012. Springer, 96-109.

HAVAEI, F., MACPHEE, M. & LEE, S. E. 2019. The effect of violence prevention strategies on perceptions of workplace safety: A study of medical-surgical and mental health nurses. *Journal of advanced nursing.*

HOCHREITER, S. & SCHMIDHUBER, J. J. N. C. 1997. Long short-term memory. 9, 1735-1780.

JHA, N. & MAHMOUD, A. MARC: A Mobile Application Review Classifier. REFSQ Workshops, 2017a.

JHA, N. & MAHMOUD, A. Mining user requirements from application store reviews using frame semantics. International working conference on requirements engineering: Foundation for software quality, 2017b. Springer, 273-287.

JHANJHI, N., BROHI, S. N. & MALIK, N. A. Proposing a Rank and Wormhole Attack Detection Framework using Machine Learning. 2019 13th International Conference on Mathematics, Actuarial Science, Computer Science and Statistics (MACS), 2019. IEEE, 1-9.

KOK, S., ABDULLAH, A., JHANJHI, N. & SUPRAMANIAM, M. 2019. Prevention of crypto-ransomware using a pre-encryption detection algorithm. *Computers,* 8, 79.

KRZYWINSKI, M., SCHEIN, J., BIROL, I., CONNORS, J., GASCOYNE, R., HORSMAN, D., JONES, S. J. & MARRA, M. A. 2009. Circos: an information aesthetic for comparative genomics. *Genome research,* 19, 1639-1645.

KUMAR, R., VARMA, H., AGRAWAL, K. & MOHANTY, B. 2001. A comprehensive study of modified Wilson plot technique to determine the heat transfer coefficient during condensation of steam and R-134a over single horizontal plain and finned tubes. *Heat Transfer Engineering,* 22, 3-12.

LATIF, R. M. A., ABDULLAH, M. T., SHAH, S. U. A., FARHAN, M., IJAZ, F. & KARIM, A. Data Scraping from Google Play Store and Visualization of its Content for Analytics. 2019 2nd International Conference on Computing, Mathematics and Engineering Technologies (iCoMET), 2019a. IEEE, 1-8.

LATIF, R. M. A., BELHAOUARI, S. B., SAEED, S., IMRAN, L. B., SADIQ, M. & FARHAN, M. 2020. Integration of Google Play Content and Frost Prediction Using CNN: Scalable IoT Framework for Big Data. *IEEE Access,* 8, 6890-6900.

LATIF, R. M. A., UMER, M., TARIQ, T., FARHAN, M., RIZWAN, O. & ALI, G. A Smart Methodology for Analyzing Secure E-Banking and E-Commerce Websites. 2019 16th International Bhurban Conference on Applied Sciences and Technology (IBCAST), 2019b. IEEE, 589-596.

LI, C., LIU, Y. & ZHAO, L. Using external resources and joint learning for bigram weighting in ilp-based multi-document summarization. Proceedings of the 2015 Conference of the North American Chapter of the Association for Computational Linguistics: Human Language Technologies, 2015. 778-787.

LIAO, J., WANG, S. & LI, D. 2019. Identification of fact-implied implicit sentiment based on multi-level semantic fused representation. *Knowledge-Based Systems,* 165, 197-207.

LINDORFER, M., VOLANIS, S., SISTO, A., NEUGSCHWANDTNER, M., ATHANASOPOULOS, E., MAGGI, F., PLATZER, C., ZANERO, S. & IOANNIDIS, S. AndRadar: fast discovery of android applications in alternative markets. International Conference on Detection of Intrusions and Malware, and Vulnerability Assessment, 2014. Springer, 51-71.

LIU, R. & ZHANG, X. 2018. Generating machine-executable plans from end-user's natural-language instructions. *Knowledge-Based Systems,* 140, 15-26.

MAALEJ, W. & NABIL, H. Bug report, feature request, or simply praise? on automatically classifying app reviews. 2015 IEEE 23rd international requirements engineering conference (RE), 2015. IEEE, 116-125.

MELLISH, C. & SUN, X. The semantic web as a linguistic resource: Opportunities for natural language generation. International Conference on Innovative Techniques and Applications of Artificial Intelligence, 2005. Springer, 77-87.

MILOSEVIC, N., DEHGHANTANHA, A. & CHOO, K.-K. R. 2017. Machine learning aided Android malware classification. *Computers & Electrical Engineering,* 61, 266-274.

OWENS, D., LOCKHART, S., MATTHEWS, D. Y. & MIDDLETON, T. J. 2019. Racial Battle Fatigue and Mental Health in Black Men. *Overcoming Challenges and Creating Opportunity for African American Male Students.* IGI Global.

PAGÁN, A., BLYTHE, H. I. & LIVERSEDGE, S. P. 2016. Parafoveal preprocessing of word initial trigrams during reading in adults and children. *Journal of Experimental Psychology: Learning, Memory, and Cognition,* 42, 411.

PANICHELLA, S., DI SORBO, A., GUZMAN, E., VISAGGIO, C. A., CANFORA, G. & GALL, H. C. Ardoc: App reviews development oriented classifier. Proceedings of the 2016 24th ACM SIGSOFT International Symposium on Foundations of Software Engineering, 2016. ACM, 1023-1027.

PURAM, N. M. & SINGH, K. An Implementation to Detect Fraud App Using Fuzzy Logic.

PURAM, N. M. & SINGH, K. R. 2018. Semantic Analysis of App Review for Fraud Detection using Fuzzy Logic.

RAMZAN, M., AWAN, S. M., ALDABBAS, H., ABID, A., FARHAN, M., KHALID, S. & LATIF, R. M. A. 2019. Internet of medical things for smart D3S to enable road safety. *International Journal of Distributed Sensor Networks,* 15, 1550147719864883.

REN, A., LIANG, C., HYUG, I., BROH, S. & JHANJHI, N. 2020. A Three-Level Ransomware Detection and Prevention Mechanism. *EAI Endorsed Transactions on Energy Web,* 7.

RORÍS, V. M. A., SABUCEDO, L. M. Á., WANDEN-BERGHE, C., GAGO, J. M. S. & SANZ-VALERO, J. 2016. Towards a mobile-based platform for traceability control and hazard analysis in the context of parenteral nutrition: description of a framework and a prototype app. *JMIR research protocols,* 5, e57.

RUAN, J., JIANG, H., LI, X., SHI, Y., CHAN, F. T. & RAO, W. 2019. A Granular GA-SVM Predictor for Big Data in Agricultural Cyber-Physical Systems. *IEEE Transactions on Industrial Informatics.*

SAEED, S., ABDULLAH, A. & JHANJHI, N. 2019. Analysis of the lung cancer patient's for data mining tool. *IJCSNS,* 19, 90.

SAEED, S., JHANJHI, N., NAQVI, M., HUMAYUN, M. & PONNUSAMY, V. 2020a. Analyzing the Performance and Efficiency of IT-Compliant Audit Module Using Clustering Methods. *Industrial Internet of Things and Cyber-Physical Systems: Transforming the Conventional to Digital.* IGI Global.

SAEED, S., JHANJHI, N., NAQVI, M., PONNUSAMY, V. & HUMAYUN, M. 2020b. Analysis of Climate Prediction and Climate Change in Pakistan Using Data Mining Techniques. *Industrial Internet of Things and Cyber-Physical Systems: Transforming the Conventional to Digital.* IGI Global.

SANGKARAN, T., ABDULLAH, A. & JHANJHI, N. 2020a. Criminal Community Detection Based on Isomorphic Subgraph Analytics. *Open Computer Science,* 10, 164-174.

SANGKARAN, T., ABDULLAH, A. & JHANJHI, N. 2020b. Criminal Network Community Detection Using Graphical Analytic Methods: A Survey. *EAI Endorsed Transactions on Energy Web,* 7.

SANTA, J., SANCHEZ-IBORRA, R., RODRIGUEZ-REY, P., BERNAL-ESCOBEDO, L. & SKARMETA, A. F. 2019. LPWAN-based vehicular monitoring platform with a generic IP network interface. *Sensors,* 19, 264.

SCHÜTTE, J., FEDLER, R. & TITZE, D. Condroid: Targeted dynamic analysis of android applications. 2015 IEEE 29th International Conference on Advanced Information Networking and Applications, 2015. IEEE, 571-578.

SINGHAL, V., JAIN, S., ANAND, D., SINGH, A., VERMA, S., RODRIGUES, J. J., JHANJHI, N. Z., GHOSH, U., JO, O. & IWENDI, C. 2020. Artificial Intelligence Enabled Road Vehicle-Train Collision Risk Assessment Framework for Unmanned Railway Level Crossings. *IEEE Access,* 8, 113790-113806.

SRINIVAS, M. 2019. Energy Efficiency in Load Balancing of Nodes Using Soft Computing Approach in WBAN. *Harmony Search and Nature Inspired Optimization Algorithms.* Springer.

TALLAT, R., LATIF, R. M. A., ALI, G., ZAHEER, A. N., FARHAN, M. & SHAH, S. U. A. Visualization and Analytics of Biological Data by Using Different Tools and Techniques. 2019 16th International Bhurban Conference on Applied Sciences and Technology (IBCAST), 2019. IEEE, 291-303.

TARIQ, T., LATIF, R. M. A., FARHAN, M., ABBAS, A. & IJAZ, F. A smart heart beat analytics system using wearable device. 2019 2nd International Conference on Communication, Computing and Digital systems (C-CODE), 2019. IEEE, 137-142.

USMANI, R. S. A., PILLAI, T. R., HASHEM, I. A. T., JHANJHI, N. & SAEED, A. 2020. A Spatial Feature Engineering Algorithm for Creating Air Pollution Health Datasets.

VIENNOT, N., GARCIA, E. & NIEH, J. A measurement study of google play. ACM SIGMETRICS Performance Evaluation Review, 2014. ACM, 221-233.

WANG, Y., LIU, H., ZHENG, W., XIA, Y., LI, Y., CHEN, P., GUO, K. & XIE, H. 2019. Multi-objective workflow scheduling with Deep-Q-network-based Multi-agent Reinforcement Learning. *IEEE Access*.

WERMKE, D., HUAMAN, N., ACAR, Y., REAVES, B., TRAYNOR, P. & FAHL, S. J. A. P. A. 2018. A Large Scale Investigation of Obfuscation Use in Google Play.

WILLIAMS, S., HARDY, C. & NITSCHKE, P. Configuring The Internet of Things (IoT): A Review and Implications for Big Data Analytics. Proceedings of the 52nd Hawaii International Conference on System Sciences, 2019.

XU, T., PENG, Q. & CHENG, Y. 2012. Identifying the semantic orientation of terms using S-HAL for sentiment analysis. *Knowledge-Based Systems,* 35, 279-289.

YANG, W., LI, J., ZHANG, Y., LI, Y., SHU, J. & GU, D. APKLancet: tumor payload diagnosis and purification for android applications. Proceedings of the 9th ACM symposium on Information, computer and communications security, 2014. 483-494.

YU, B., XU, Z.-B. & LI, C.-H. 2008. Latent semantic analysis for text categorization using neural network. *Knowledge-Based Systems,* 21, 900-904.

ZHANG, F., HUANG, H., ZHU, S., WU, D. & LIU, P. ViewDroid: Towards obfuscation-resilient mobile application repackaging detection. Proceedings of the 2014 ACM conference on Security and privacy in wireless & mobile networks, 2014. ACM, 25-36.

ZHOU, W., ZHOU, Y., GRACE, M., JIANG, X. & ZOU, S. Fast, scalable detection of piggybacked mobile applications. Proceedings of the third ACM conference on Data and application security and privacy, 2013. ACM, 185-196.

RANA M. AMIR LATIF received the B.S.C.S. degree from COMSATS University Islamabad Sahiwal, Sahiwal, Pakistan. He is graduated in M.S. degree from COMSATS University Islamabad Sahiwal, Sahiwal, Pakistan. He is currently doing job as a Lecture in Barani Institute of Sciences, Sahiwal. He also had worked as a Lecture of Computer Science at the Quaid-e-Azam College of Engineering and Technology, Sahiwal for about one years. He is also a Research Assistant with the Department of Computer Science, CUI, under the supervision of Dr. M. Farhan. He has many research publications in high impact factor journals also he has many publications in well reputed international conferences. He is also doing a funded project with the government of Pakistan in national research program for universities. His research interests include machine learning, data sciences, and the IoT.

Dr MUHAMMAD FARHAN received the B.S.C.S. degree from the Virtual University of Pakistan (VU), in 2007, the M.S.C.S. degree from the University of Management and Technology (UMT), Pakistan, in 2010, and the Ph.D. degree in computer science from the Department of Computer Sciences and Engineering, University of Engineering and Technology (UET), Pakistan, in 2017. He had worked as a Lecturer in Department of Computer Science, COMSATS University Islamabad Sahiwal, Sahiwal, Pakistan. He also had worked as an Instructor of Computer Science at the Virtual University of Pakistan for about five years. He is currently an Assistant Professor with the Department of Computer Science, COMSATS University Islamabad, Sahiwal. He started his research career with the publication of a conference paper in San Luis Potosí, Mexico, IEEE CPS. He has honored for winning travel grant provided by ACM and Microsoft for the presentation of a student paper in the ACM/SIGAPP Symposium (Human Computer Interaction track) held by the University of Salamanca, Spain. He has published a good number of SCI-indexed impact factor journal articles, which are published by the Journal of Real- Time Image Processing by Springer, Multimedia Tools and Applications by Springer, the International Journal of Distributed Sensor Networks by SAGE Journals, the EURASIA Journal of Mathematics, Science and Technology Education by MODESTUM, Life Science Journal by Marshland Press and in various renowned journals of IEEE, Springer, Elsevier, and Hindawi. His research interests include data science, machine and deep learning, and the Internet of Things.

Prof. Dr. Khalid Hussain received his MS IT degree in 1996 from Preston University Islamabad. He did M.S. CS from COMSATS Institute of Information Technology Islamabad in 2007 specializing in Wireless Communication and Networks. He received his Ph.D. from Universiti Tecknolotgi Malaysia specializing Wireless Networks Security.

Dr Noor Zaman Jhanjhi is currently working as Associate Professor with Taylor's University Malaysia. He has great international exposure in academia, research, administration, and academic quality accreditation. He worked with ILMA University, and King Faisal University (KFU) for a decade. He has 20 years of teaching & administrative experience. He has an intensive background of academic quality accreditation in higher education besides scientific research activities, he had worked a decade for academic accreditation and earned ABET accreditation twice

132

for three programs at CCSIT, King Faisal University, Saudi Arabia. He also worked for National Commission for Academic Accreditation and Assessment (NCAAA), Education Evaluation Commission Higher Education Sector (EECHES) formerly NCAAA Saudi Arabia, for institutional level accreditation. He also worked for the National Computing Education Accreditation Council (NCEAC).

Dr Noor Zaman has awarded as top reviewer 1% globally by WoS/ISI (Publons) recently for the year 2019. He has edited/authored more than 13 research books with international reputed publishers, earned several research grants, and a great number of indexed research articles on his credit. He has supervised several postgraduate students, including master's and PhD. Dr Noor Zaman Jhanjhi is an Associate Editor of IEEE ACCESS, moderator of IEEE TechRxiv, Keynote speaker for several IEEE international conferences globally, External examiner/evaluator for PhD and masters for several universities, Guest editor of several reputed journals, member of the editorial board of several research journals, and active TPC member of reputed conferences around the globe.

 **Dr Mamoona Humayun** has completed her PhD. in Computer Architecture from Harbin Institute of Technology, China. She has 12 years of teaching and administrative experience internationally. She is an active reviewer for a series of journals. She has supervised various master's and Ph.D. thesis. Her research interests include Global software development, requirement engineering, knowledge management, Cyber Security, and wireless sensor networks.

Publisher: Eliva Press SRL

Email: info@elivapress.com